John Welch

Also by John Welch:

Poetry:
A Place Like Here (Katabasis, London 1968)
Six of Five (The Many Press, London 1975)
Wanting To Be Here (The X Press, London 1976)
The Fish God Problem (The Many Press, London 1977)
Braiding the Squadron (The Many Press, London 1977)
And Ada Ann, A Book of Narratives
           (Great Works Press, Bishops Stortford 1978)
Performance (The Many Press, London 1979)
Grieving Signal (The Many Press, London 1980)
The Storms / Lip Service (The Many Press, London 1980)
Out Walking (Anvil, London 1984)
Erasures (The Many Press, London 1991)
Blood and Dreams (Reality Street Editions, London 1991)
Its Radiance (Poetical Histories, Cambridge 1993)
Glyph (Grille, London 1995)
Greeting Want (infernal methods, Cambridge 1997)
The Eastern Boroughs (Shearsman Books, Exeter 2004)
British Estate (AARK Arts, London & Delhi 2004)
On Orkney (infernal methods. Stromness 2005)

Prose
Dreaming Arrival (Shearsman Books, Exeter, 2008)

As editor:
Stories from South Asia (Oxford University Press, 1984)

John Welch

Collected Poems
1970-2007

Shearsman Books
Exeter

Published in the United Kingdom in 2008 by
Shearsman Books Ltd
58 Velwell Road
Exeter EX4 4LD

ISBN 978-1-905700-57-8

Copyright © John Welch, 1970-2008

The right of John Welch to be identified as the author of this work has been asserted by him in accordance with the Copyrights, Designs and Patents Act of 1988. All rights reserved. No part of this publication may be reproduced, stored in a retrieval system, transmitted in any form or by any means, electronic, mechanical, photocopying, recording or otherwise, without the prior permission of the publisher.

Contents

Foreword   9

Out Walking
It and You   12
The Readers   13
Poem   13
Treaty   14
Circles   15
Conference   15
Halt   16
Voice   16
Mysterious Griefs   17
On Swansea Beach   18
Clearway   19
Undercliff Walk   20
Old People's Home   21
Walking Out   22
Out Walking   30
Here and There   31
At Hammersmith Flyover   32
A Walk in Autumn   33
A Walk in Winter   34
Twenty Sonnets   35
Noon   45
The Polished Grain   46
With a Sigh of Amazement She . . .   49
Grieving Signal   52
Lip Service   55
Snow in April   59
Dreams Dreams   60
Braiding the Squadron   62
Buddleia   65
Five Preludes   69

Dust Settled
The Explosion   76
National Curriculum   77
Lucy Cheryl and Charles   78

And Ada Ann	82
Helen and John	88
The Brood of Fiction	91
The Bush of Growth	97
Again Again	99
Diurnal	101
Not Half: The Sixties	115
Panels	117
Pictures for the City	122
Letter Follows	124
Mourning	126
Estuary and Dune	127
In Lieu of a Preface	130

BLOOD AND DREAMS

The Fish God	132
Dragon Dreaming	137
Dreaming the Sign	142
Local Aspects	150
Fresco	166
The Shame of the Oracle	168
That Night	173
Our Mirrors	175
Imagination and Dream	179
Mackerel Sky	185

THE CONCRETE SHRINE

A Vigil	188
The Storms	201
On Skye	207
The Concrete Shrine	210
What He Said	215
On Orkney	223
Opening	235
Birth Right	239
For Joachim	242
Out	243

GREETING WANT

Night Music	250

In Dalston	250
Taking Refuge	251
News Time	252
White Lilac	253
For The Births	254
The Pear Tree	255
Voyage	257
The Flaying Of Marsyas	258
Days	259
Erasures	262
Seven Dawns	271
Iris	276
Bird Talk	283
Shades	291
Laurel	294
Found	296
The Vine	298
Its Radiance	299
Laila	311
Glyph	315
Poor	320
Greeting Want	324

THE EASTERN BOROUGHS

Art / Work	328
Creature	328
Chartres	329
Bungalow: 'La-Mer'	330
Edge	332
Out Walking, Again	333
Orfeo	334
It Was	336
Missing Plinth	337
Exhibit	338
Lanyon at St Ives	339
Authored	340
The Feelings	342
The Good Things	343
Deaf	346
Language Lesson	347

At the Centre	349
Dig	352
Shores	356
Family	362
Fathering	363
A Place Like Here	371
Turning	400
Hunger And Thirst	401
Analysis	403
Patient	404
Lyric	405
The Moments	409
Launched	411
At Watch	413
Rose Mirror	414
The Eastern Boroughs	416
Gallery	421
Benign Tumour	422
Swift	423
Lake	424
Breathe, Then	425
I Is	427
Mirrored	428

THE WIND HARP

Aeolian	430
Textbridge	430
Coasting	431
Collected	433
Visiting Silence	435
Personal Poem	441
Portrait	443
Weymouth Sands	444
Beached	445
Star Fish	446
As If Where	447
Drop Dead	448
Mask	449
Just A Touch	450
The Thing About	451

Foreword

I started writing in 1957. However virtually none of this earliest work, and there was a great deal of it, is included here. I retain a certain affection for these poems, a fair number of which appeared in magazines during the 1960s, but have decided not to include them.

The poems collected here in the section 'Dust Settled' date from the early 1970s. Some of them are taken from *And Ada Ann*, published by Great Works Press in 1978; some are previously uncollected. The work in the sections *Out Walking* (Anvil, 1984), *Blood and Dreams* (Reality Street, 1991), *Greeting Want* (infernal methods, 1997) and *The Eastern Boroughs* (Shearsman, 2004) is broadly what was contained in the four collections so titled, though with some revisions and a few poems removed altogether. *The Vigil* and *A Place Like Here* contain work dating mainly from the late 1970s through to the early 1990s and previously uncollected. The final section, *The Wind Harp,* is recent, uncollected work.

My acknowledgements and heartfelt thanks to Peter Philpott, Peter Jay, Ken Edwards and Nigel Wheale, publishers of these collections, and to others, publishers and editors too numerous to list here, who have shown faith in my work over the years. My special thanks go to Tony Frazer of Shearsman for undertaking this *Collected Poems*, as well as having been the publisher of my most recent full-length collection.

Out Walking

It and You

It is all a question of distance,
of how far you stand, and at what angle
to the subject
                which is

the constant sense of bafflement
birds singing   in the grey garden
a fir tree heavy with raindrops
outside the
                kitchen door, smell of
                herbs
thriving in the damp soil. Turn
back in the door's shadow,
the birds sing reasonably
not like you   there is
nothing else for it

when the sky pours and raindrops
crawl over the huge glass.
It is somewhere to one side of you
your speech depends on this distance
this angle.
              In the morning sunlight
peonies thrive, in front gardens,
their heads heavy with water.

The Readers

The turkey lay on a slab on its back
The neck hanging down
And over its eyes was a cap of paper.
Echoes of slaughter
Cut across city wind. Their heads
Stuffed into our pockets our lives
Are becoming a legend.
In spite of this we embrace our food,
We absorb, we include, we incorporate
Then ponder the pages, engrossed in lamplight.

Poem

The beautiful guts are arranged in trays
And a solemn moment of weighing.
I climb up the stairs holding the bag of blood.
He has sealed it with crimson tape.

My body stretched in the bath like a coffin
Is a lonely flower. Preparing this meat
To music of Bach I trim off the gristle.
The liver falls raggedly apart.

TREATY

I go across London to meet you. It's more than a year now
Since we parted. Where I pause on the railway bridge
There is a peculiar quiet, only one child shouting
From the back of a house, and a cold sun shining.
After a week of migraines, you are better you say,
Doped and smiling, smelling of soap and tiredness.
The new sun is a rose rooted in valium.
You tell me about your boyfriends, how silly they are,
I try to explain how it is now with my writing
But I do not speak of your pictures face to the wall.
You draw your hair out in front of the fire
To dry it, already it glitters with silver.
You ask if it's dry. I feel it, it's like
Hay in a summer wind, and when we go out together
Past twenty four sphinxes lining one side of the hill,
Walking into the wind, we both feel weak, we are like ghosts
Returning to a meal that went cold an age ago.
We eat wisely, we do not quarrel, for this is
Ghost food we are eating, sunshine and smiles –
Our smiles mixing together in sharp winter weather.
As you turn to leave me, stepping off from the pavement
Perhaps I'll remember this day above all our others
As something withdrawn from time, like one card from the pack,
This peculiar quiet, only one child shouting
From the back of a house, and a cold sun shining.

Circles

You draw a circle round yourself.
You say, "Step in, but carefully –
Mind how you go, that's better."

I am a row of trees.
You are the sun on me.

You go into the wallpaper
Disguising yourself among the roses.

As I lie in bed in the morning
Light heaving against the curtains
Your face settles on mine like a gentle mask.

Tonight two bodies in league
Will imitate the sea.

Conference

The lift whispers, far far
It takes them.

The static crackles in carpets
Under their careful dubious tread.

The voices glide like water.
Their hands are soft as flowers

While money flows
Under their feet in a hidden river.

Halt

"You ought to get out more often." It came
From the far side of an ear,
 "You ought to live there, behind the trees,
Where the sky is." A bird,
Crossing the air, brakes gently.

Voice

Along the line of roof a builder
Pushes his barrow of afternoon.
The street below is dusted with pronouns.

Wind carves a statue. Listen –
Out of ourselves, our selves: a telephone
Wakes, and our voices

Rub together, like grasshoppers.
A rusty bird starts up. A city
Is rising over the ruined fields.

We shelter in its shade.

Mysterious Griefs

Hills sleep, what else? Since the water
Retreated, eyes rest on them. We woke
To a window, sheltering trees.
We crossed the hills. Walls hurried past.
The birds arose like ghosts of souls
From field and branch. We followed valleys,
Slept on the beach, awoke to the same
Unending stretch of water. Mortality,
Its origin, bright patch, mysterious
Griefs, the implements
At a field's edge, waggons lithe
And springy as boats. One grey day
Our maps spotted with rain
We came to a camp, a small dark hill
Beyond a concrete farm. The grass
Blurred but revealed the fort's outline.
Air was thick with ancestors, here and
Nowhere, mysterious griefs, their bodies
Gone past all reckoning, the way a path
Just ends in sky. Hills slept.
Each day we set out from our village.
Your dress moved like a piece of the silence.
A gap on the hill's brow where the road went
Held all distances, sea stirred somewhere
Beyond. Together we crossed the hills.
Wheat thickened within the ripening hour.

On Swansea Beach

Along the hill's spine
Ran a row of houses like teeth
Where curtained windows guarded
Collections of furniture, flowers.

In the refreshment pavilion
The orders come endlessly:
"One orange squash. Two teas."
Always the same, but never
Exactly –
        Where did we learn
Such discipline, silence and care?

It was dusk on the sandflats
Sea half a mile out, and
Invisible now, a
Line of sound like a wire
Stretched across darkness.

I walked between
The waiting sea, the saw-backed hills
Hearing the intermittent
Murmur of gulls.

"Creation and destruction:
Shiva holds them apart
And the beauty of his movement
Is the beginning and end of all things."

Clearway

To begin with, you crossed
Ripening hills. A pencil of monument,
Set against sky, disappeared and the
Runners went past in a frieze.

A shower of rain in the valley spattered
A gatepost, lion among leaves –
You then reached a middle range
At about three, a domestic entrance.

You shifted. The fuchsia leaned heavily
By the rosemary bush. You were careful
Not to leave mud on the carpet.
This was another good day

Of sailing, the weather safe behind glass.
You opened an atlas, a gazetteer.
There was always a smell of earth
Beside the shed door recurring.

While lorries swayed over the hillsides
In a queue leaving the coasts
With their freight. The undefended
Roads went quiet and corn slumbered

And the same sky as in childhood
Rose behind, like a curtain,
But always changing. We are here
Days, hours, minutes without number –

Outcrops of flesh, that keep reappearing.

Undercliff Walk

Walking along
The concrete path that runs
Between the cliffs and the sea
We read in the rock-face
Strata of history
In many-coloured
Layers of rock, in fossils
Settled in stone, heart of our world
Gone hard and alien,
While on the small patch of beach
That shrinks hourly without ever
Quite disappearing
People are throwing stones,
Are dressing, undressing
Eating, drinking and laughing,
Making love. The sea
Is grey like the sky
And darkens towards the horizon,
Moves only a little
As it sighs on the beach.

Old People's Home

The place appears
Next to a school
Of voices. Visits are rare
Though there is often
In the streets a kind of
Amateur music.
One waves. You might say royal,
A smile, the elbow
On a low sill.
Some spindly
Institutional shrubs
Are anchored in this
London dust. My life
Passes here daily. Nobody
Needs to know, where a
Wide-eyed death leans in.
Again she turns away
From the enormous window
Called back to her distances –
A bundle of garments that
Shifts in a corridor
Away from this
Wall of fused sand
Where reflections pursue
Reflections, and mine among them.

Walking Out

A voice shouts reggae
In the cold and blowy distance

To begin with distance. A wall
Drops straight down on the street
Is here and now, and where you are
Quite still, too busy breathing.

Careful solidity of your dreams.

In the middle distance
The ruined Sundays rubbed together

And a great sermon of the trees.

A long way away, you will see the bodies begin.

We are moisture, today
The grey and the dry.
Burnt grass is a sign
In the park, and the scarce pronoun
Is hollowed out. Remains of trees
Fill rooms, burn as coal or oil.
Everywhere
The trees go on in the sky

To keep it on the point of the flame, until
Rinsed of anger, sorrow and pity
Melodramas obsess the gap, reach stasis
The performers are the clock, distilled focus
Watching us go over our sofas like clouds

    Getting out
These walls/curtains, where my skin cracked with psoriasis
Joins me to the things of the world.

Language the snare
The city: a name
Rising up and looking down on it
The illustrations are running down off the page

Trapped on the pavement, pausing among the movement

Each day I go out and do this thing
Called 'work'
While light streams out and in, images
Hide in the eye

Losing, renouncing
Disappearing into the conversation
The blood finds its way, warily.

The long waving arms of the buddleia
Attract insects
To a landscape of 'inner city decay'

We enjoy the same battered hungers
Dancing out the message of nectar –
The horn, and the labial

Brushing their way through the market,
Chickens piled high
And nearby, the webby shade

Guts dropped into a tub

The old Chinese lady
Dips in her hand, so
Neatly
Pulls out the chicken-legs
Wipes the end of her fingers

Such distance, such closeness.

Aeroplanes disappear
Into the fold of their coming.
Beached Cadillacs rot in the weather.

Round here people hammer cars
Perched perilously on bricks.
They do not shape their journeys.

Something called 'the country'
Is earthed up around the exits. But first
The dive into leafier suburbs –
A labyrinth of wealth

Exile into exile, lifting back.
The children in their Rastafari colours.

Behind corrugated iron
Here is a field
Flourishing, ragwort and willow-herb.

A silver cross
Swings at his ear, a girl on each arm
A silver skeleton
Jangles in the parked car –
Those who don't know
The car is the fetish.

Dogs defend ruined gardens
And our park is barely renewed
Out of its dust.

At home you are quiet.

Nearer the church, lime trees thicken
To a darkness full of weak insects
The pavement beneath is sticky and grubby

Resting with shopping bags
Squatting on a step

Here there is something archaic
Imperfect and nearly destroyed and
Ready to be broken

Jah music

Sun in its trough in its nest.

At six o'clock, faces
Say more than their words
Could ever do. In the bar

They are masked in sunlight.
Eye hollows seem to darken
Like valleys in shadow.
Playing pool the balls are enclosed
In a careful triangle. Outside
It was slabs of
Concrete resting on dirt,
The convolvulous threading its way
Among herb robert and dock.
Buddleia brushes against
Corrugations. In evening sunlight
The town's an abrupt memory.

All quiet the site
Lorries and other gear marooned in dust

L'OREAL faded shopcard brown with age

The feathery tired plants
Each price is like a noose

The street is its transactions
And nothing final. She pauses
On a balcony of wind, in gritty air
Her pavement is
The edge of nothing

Fibres loosen and pause
Wallpaper flaps like a curtain
Weightless traffic
A row of doors boards up the site

As the fire died down
Even the flames laid back their ears
In the charred timbers and seemed to sleep.

They smartened the premises
Working all night all weekend
Tending a tree of money

In this late age

But do not shake its whispers down.

Sparrows have whitened the pavement
Where they roost in their fan-shaped sycamore.
Arranging information in patterns
I listen for the humming of the codes.
Political lies storm the hoardings.

Shorn of a hand – the stump is
Describing circles in the air –
I end up at the mirror's point of rest,
Helplessness of what is. In an ornate
Public house, alcohol's truth
Vomited up in front of a mirror.

Camping among the ruins; the dazed municipality.
The amputated
Blunder through our city air.

The wind-based sky
Is our surface of origin

Beside shaved bowling-greens
I eat a chilly lunch.
Wind massages my paper bag

Sparrows shave the budding twigs
And chirp in a fat chorus.
Later the tennis courts, erotic trouble,
The life of middle age.

The coffee a burnt taste round the heart.
The pinewoods were a sort of blue,
The sun a pale drop, smoke of cloud
And then it settled into something brighter.
Now evening brushes the sky clean
Leaves a few small vivid clouds like plates
Suspended in the blue: Kings Cross.

Lights come on from under our eyelids.
Our bus ambles through the urban twilight.

Frantic pursuit of the actual
The meat is so far from the animal
Ah there you are in tears and wonder

You are your own breath on the glass
Among the borrowed repetitions
You are the reader
In the centre, unique, privileged, certain.

Statements: the surface
Is full of interest

With the addition of signs
The names of my children
My voice is taken out of your mouth
A city twinkles through its fumes
Or even reddened hills
Surround a lung of brass.
A still grey afternoon. A few
Drops of rain are thrown about
A dust of insects salts the air
In the hollow grassy lane. Some pressure
Hangs like a curtain, primes these buds.

We skim the fields.

We persevere, as if about to locate
Some enormous exhaustion, far out ahead.

An event meets an unshakeable barrier.
Fracture helps it grow. We
Stutter in broken sentences
Phrases of imagination, erotic
Miseries. Light writes itself
Round towers and whispers,
The cloud-bright windy day. How long
Can you hope to fend off meaning?

Smaller amounts and fragrant demands,

Another twilight thick with birdsong.

Out Walking

Standing at the edge
Of the park you have
The distant slowly moving
Figures to guide you,
Dark in the sunlight
Two of them in the centre
In confabulation. This is
The way in to the picture
Except that it isn't a picture.
There are pigeons dotted
On the slope of a roof
Huddled out of the wind
But I return to
The same inscribed figures
These commonplace streets
Have brought me to.
A train goes by at one edge
And wails on two notes like a bird
Some voices of children rise
Out of a well of indifference,
The morning, October
The rails are running with light
Deserted platforms, the horn
Of plenty the world and my walking
Is variously inscribed
Upon it. Still talking
The two men
Have moved off across the grass.

Here and There

The face by the bar is old, composed
To patience, in a backwash of waiting

Skull in front of a mirror that reads
'A Gift to Bill and Iris'

A door opened, half of the street came in
Reflected all at once in the flinty writing

Ah emptiness that you can never find
All round you. Feet take it somewhere

A used-up glare of petunias
In their shallow concrete bowl

The hebe opened in a polite border
Clouds moved swiftly across –

The deep buried sparkle
A child imparts to its days.

AT HAMMERSMITH FLYOVER

Something to balance it on
Pale stalks of road.
A fence runs by the kerb
To keep the two apart
A principle of escape
Operates, on a tonsil
Of vomit and spit, washed away
By the operations of dawn
While the cantilevered gutters
Carry away some space
Each person's is separate, clear
Out of here past the flapping
Wallpaper's faded foliage before
A shocking sky. Town
Suspended from wires, an asphalt
Butterfly, the insistent
Soft explosions of collapse.
Cross your legs over the cushion
Of cloud, to begin before starting.
These were optimistic words
A trapped button of root –
Out of here, out of here
The shopping arcades arose one morning
Like our blind music.

A Walk in Autumn

To have that kind of faith
In the language,
Today fading curiously
Into pediments, tower-blocks
Fringing the park's table –
Trying to gather them in
The polished table flares in the sun,
On it the prim violet.
This is the prelude, the before setting-out.
Looked at in the mirror upstairs
I quite obviously have substance
The ground all round me beaten flat.
Exploratory, edging forward
Down the same faded streets of promises
My footsteps are still the visible
Under pale blue skies that we cherish
And a little sunlight coming again
To burnish the tops of the cars.

A Walk in Winter

Among rough winter rubbish
The hellebore arrives.
The memorials meanwhile
Are passionate with saying.
Up Chestnut Avenue, and that's
The end of that –
'To the Thermal Clinic'.
Here at the terminus
The silver trains are corralled.
Shrubs planted by the railway
Bear whitish clusters
Even in midwinter.
Elsewhere December spoils the buds
And all round's padded with directions.
We pass by laurel and fir.
Sunlight crisps their deckled
Edges in fits and starts.
Meanwhile turning another page
Indoors a clock discreetly
Chimes, some leaves
Blown inward into the hall
Await the little storm
Of our return.

Everything in the City

Everything in the city comes to this table.
There must be something to be said about these
Explosions of laughter at the stairhead,
Rumours of approach in the tunnels.
Water is scattered in the air, everywhere
Attesting to the importance of clouds
And the weather changes every few hours
Where blind men are making journeys over the city
Tapping trees and observing the shadow
Sound casts. Processions are crossing it
Bearing advertisements.
Essential oils fry in the pan. "Bury it in
An inch of water, it will sing for five minutes."
Everything in the city comes to this table.

Morning Was Best

Morning was best. At midnight because of the heat
The windows stand open. He rises renewed from the bath.
His clothes are drying outside on the balcony.
He is tired of the clutter he picks his way through.
Once he was loved, but he makes little progress.
He looks out. A woman is standing
Beside her window, smoking a last cigarette.
On the city's far side, under sodium light,
A unicorn rears, and goods are displayed
In shop windows, bright and silent.
Dossers are settling down for the night
By the river in a rustle of newspaper.
Sleep comes slowly, like a child led into the city
And their bodies exhale a strange quiet.

The Waste of It

The waste of it, my skin that makes too many
Cells. It's called psoriasis. I lay
Under a sunlamp in a hospital.
Nurses were busy around, trying to right
The balance, skilled in such wars. The waste
As when the fish scatters its eggs in millions.
On the street corner a broken artery flowers.
A network of veins and roads covers the mind.
Morning was ebbing away. Then cars
Changed gear, asserting continuity.
I dived through the crowd like a swimmer, I was not
Part of it. At night I bathed, emerging
Free of its taint. Each dawn I raise
My body to the mirror of the morning.

On the Way to the Park

The banked-up clouds and the exploding leaves.
We are refugees from silence
In the street of valves and whistles
Where flutes and cage-birds celebrate distress.
In cracks some plant life flourishes –
Look, the tough flower, and now the park
Of animals being named, lost cries from Eden,
Each plaque, each map a small grave-tablet
Clipped to the wire. Birds preen themselves
thrown against the bars like insects
While in the street
The more successful species parades.
Between the two, I stroll beneath the trees.
Some sunlight finds its way into the blond pages.

Hydrangea

Hydrangea before the flats has flowered –
This gross bush, reddish and purple like a face.
Upright in bars as if beneath far skies
Men drink alone, stern-faced, and look away.
Home, and I water the garden again
Then dine off a round table, not feeling well.
Laying the face on the face this language
Is a scandal, and I'm its shadow
Walking slowly into the future tense.
There is no freedom anywhere but here.
Lie down in it, it can't last. Drought
Is lasting. Half a life
Is better than none at all. The drinkers rise.
Hydrangea of the flats, how parched your ground!

Habitual Insolence

Habitual insolence the streets encourage:
Flexing the muscles before daybreak,
The ones little used, then passed by hands
Over the flat and the vertical areas
Gazing into the eyes of approaching motorists
Who gnaw the wheel accommodating miles.
The muscle halts by here
In its cultivated rags mid splinters
Of the valuable flask, lapsed cloths of sunlight.
Being calm under an always turning heel
I am the wax archangel and the
Catalogue of cars, the useless rain
Leans inward past impenetrable churches,
These stone valves blackening down the years.

Movement

I, knocked off its table,
And the rest of you float past, leading a
Submarine life, as when the ship
Is sinking through strata of water
Touching bottom so gently in a cloud
Of sand. It settles for generations.
Tenants move in, encrusting it
With their homes. So through the city
Carefully, looking for bottom, you place two cups
On the counter's exact centre, this being the one
Stipulation. The trains beneath you are
Speeding towards it, and outside are secretaries,
Their breasts swelling with virtue, but you
Haven't touched it, you haven't begun to touch it.

City Twilight

Is he experienced, out of this swarm of nothings?
He is being drawn softly in
To a network of dark intentions. Pedestrians
Gnaw at the street, their bone of history,
Once voluble, and now fallen silent.
The corrugated iron is afloat with shadows.
A newcomer here looks carefully round
As he closes the door, sniffs the stars before going.
He wanted to master this brilliance
That we are the emblems of, a street and a room.
Inside, a landscape opens out like a fan
Over his table: afternoons: rising like smoke
To greet his oppressors. No, it is only history
As a wind blows out of the evening carrying voices.

A Great Heat

A great heat. As if that wasn't enough,
A bouquet of words, the sly honeysuckle
Perpetrating its remembered hedgerows
And love-affairs. Vinous roses moreover
Were staggering in front gardens, and pale
Hydrangeas that hadn't been watered with chemical.
As if that wasn't enough. But this is a
People who like flowers, as au pairs notice
Approving for once. The gardens stretch
Across this land like shares in Paradise,
Unthinkingly planted, carefully tamed.
Words invade them, people with names.
Why? A great heat. The city stinks,
Sounds ripening on a branch of thought.

One a.m.

One a.m., a cat is floating between
The curtain and window. Her thighs
Close. The city is full of sleepers
And hurtling cars. There are blocks
Of flesh to begin it, and later the huge
Parabola, with jewels hanging down,
A ring on a finger, the shine of a tear
Crawling over the yawning page.
One o'clock, the cat is well cared for, would
Rather be hunting, and I remember
All that I am tonight, hurrying
Home. The problem is, we are all
Separately loved, are we
More than this each, this passed-on-a-plate?

So Long

Leaning so long over myself, each
Day the same, the honey-coloured landscape
Of shuttered summers; today at lunchtime
I followed tree-trunks bare with sunlight.
Beside a ditch, two children, and beyond them
The factories and the football pitches.
Here the doubtful river was being cleansed,
Each pool covered in gulls. This is the dull seed
From which it will germinate, this nothing-at-all,
Sunlight suddenly trapped in the classroom's
High windows, rain-wet roads, and in my heart
The Buddhas of a thousand years. Today
As I stand beneath a cold sky, there is one Alsatian
Weaving over these empty, cared-for fields.

Supper

Nothing more but to gorge
And disgorge. The herring I had fell apart
Like a book, collapsing into this heap of flesh,
Delicate, just a shade oily,
Full of eggs. Wind blew the sycamore pale.
I dined alone off a round table
Feeling ill, then you called me.
But away from you the beds were sterile,
A memory, curtains filling and resting,
The city of breath, eight million people sighed,
The phone still snoozing in its black silence.
Tomorrow I'll see you again, meanwhile
I'm the coat we both saw from the back
Disappearing along the street.

The Root Swayed

The root swayed and air foundered.
Withered sunlight was part of the performance.
I was the ruined preface, your body grammar
Played at here and there in the sycamore shade.
Shut in the hull of the sphere
You and I were the dust of a tune.
Our new clothes waited in a box, were fresh
To be donned after sex, when we shall
Assume new personality robes
To stand on a tongue of the sunlight
Sipping our cautious drinks, and be.
The slow oil of what I was
Sank, we were encouraged though nervous
And our ears pricked up, like corn sown to a drumbeat

Afternoons

The afternoon's for fantasy. We walk
Up and down inside ourselves. A washed-out
Purple rose is by the front door.
Everywhere mothers watch their children
In rows of gardens, gather food from shops.
Before each house are varied flowers
And women with the names of flowers,
Eyes heavy on the edge of greeting.
Shaping meals, they chop and blend,
Break and create. Their selves like garments
Swirl round the stem of a body, unnamed,
Secret, half-remembered in fantasy.
These are renewed, are troubled, age
Faded mothers who stir in their blooms.

For the Paintings of Morris Louis

Our day began on a dull red door
Hammering on to a curtain to open.
Veils and diseases. Our torn halts
Covered the ground in a fury of colour.
There was stitching on the duck surface,
The little bumps of different coloured hills.
The great underneath uprose. We quietly
Admired its huge berg infested with colour
Till we were ourselves surface, envying surface.
Leaving the massive acres of islands
We sank in, becoming colour poured on
And were buried up to the knees. We waded,
Ran and ran across white space tilted.
We were the enormous air around, comprehending.

Butterfly Bush

Desert forage, sky like a primrose
Yoking together the violent distances.
I had observed the boles of trees.
All was faded, our forest ending
In upright silence, my face recovered,
s alert by a bush of lyrics.
Now through the strict performance
Of gardens butterflies staggered.
At the desert's reversed centre
Air was charged with their silence.
The sun blazed into a jug. We moved
Into a ring of knowledge.
Secure on the carpet, the smoke
Returned, like memory.

Unknown Soldier

The unknown soldier lay in a wood
Next to some ants. A beige colonel
Arrived, and a casket. There were eyes
Trapped under glass, while everyone else's
Dried in the wind, an insect distress.
Their loud morality spoke –
The soap of multitudes, sounds
Of brushed hair, and the windless arch
Of the sky was broken again.
Memory thumped on the wood's green table.
Her hands roamed over the cards, till daybreak
Rubbed light on the vast horizons,
A fur of inscriptions – and look, the clock
Still talks to itself in a brightening room.

End of the War

The shades were appeased, and the bodies
Remaining still walked about
Tottering on their heels, under the
Sky's wheel, and in its blue cave
The gunfire crackled and echoed.
Fortunate officers went into hiding
Till doom discovered their rumpled beds,
Sky dark on a table. For three
Mornings this general lay in his room
Like a penitent judge, watching murderers
Pile up outside his window, and as he departed
The sky came up to him
Walking on its hands, where there had been
Bombs waiting in the air like phases of history.

The Drops of Wind

The sunlight brought them out, this bunch
Of aliens, tulips in their beds, striped pals,
Foreign students studying in the parks,
Huddled in deckchairs. Ach your wezzair ...
Tiring it is to have to gather
The drops of wind. Yoko was telling us
About the cherry trees in her land.
Fractured grace and lyric wind
Still proved bothersome. The Underground
Was full of songsters whistling to guitars.
The clouds glowed darkly. Later, clearing skies
Turned pale blue, early evening. Someone's mother
Was bending down to say hello like lilac.
On the wind's blunt knife our blossoms cooled.

For the Third Time

For the third time he is visiting China.
Most of the people are idolaters.
Excellent rhubarb grows in the mountains.
The musk deer is found in the region round Erginul
At the full moon, a bag of coagulated
Blood or imposthume forms in the stomach.
They cut out the membrane by moonlight.
The Khan had five hundred women from Ungut
Selected each year, but rejected any
That snored, or had halitosis. Did the Ungutians mind?
Of course not, they deemed it an honour and when
He returned no one believed him,
Until he ripped open his coat
And showed them the rhubarb packed inside.

Noon

The sun's operations are singularly loud.
It goes buzz every time you approach.
At midday it goes even darker, at the
Centre. Shining through crystals
It makes a halo, peeling the eyes
As it expands. Discussing the eyes
We kiss at noon, dryness, explosions,
False-scorpions munching, already
The desk grows bright at the edges.

The Polished Grain

When the last of the authors had been folded back
Into the ground, and the ground was clean again
The last of them having been removed

Sinking back into the quilted mud

There were trees heaped around the window, a garden
Beginning to fill with children, whose voices were
Pale as straw. Who were thinking.

It was clean as hunger, then.
A speck of sand came, disturbing the lens
It cracked, receded
And faded into a smile.

Binoculars on a sill
Regarded the trees, tennis.

Binocular orifice, composed rock
The light being polished where it bounced
The grain being polished. It was called
Understanding Everything.

The names were names of names.
Streets were full of them.
They entered me like darkness.
They were deciduous.
My body was bent, like this.
Many entered me, I was between

Doors, so to speak, like
Leaves the doors grew and flourished.

In the polished sky a buzzard
And a cloud shaped like a shark.
In the polished sky an advertisement,

A block going into the azure.
In the polished sky the meanings
Gathered like statues, filling apertures

Their whippy little letters
Grouped thickly together. At the

Table's corner meanwhile some kind of
Metal instrument flashed.
The table humped its back

The darkness of its table all concentrated
Into this darkness to resist
The encroachment of sky.
It silently withered and was told.

The throat shuts, its
Conversations remember
Windows, horizons.

The table is sore with sky. Wind rubs
Things float across the eye

Like bits of paper in the sly air.
They rustle as they touch
The surface of a lens perched on a sill.
We're all included
Since most of us know how to float.

Whose are the houses, the mirror, the clothes?
The flapping line, whose?

In the empty sky / in the last bit of azure.

With a Sigh of Amazement She...

A sigh of amazement. "Well really" she said. Flop, flop, flop the bare boards. "I don't know why this humming. We've had trouble with the taps and the telephone as well." Flop, flop, flop. "Look, isn't the garden a mess, 1 don't know how we'll ever get it right, and that furniture..." A bird heads off into the silent clouds. "Well no, really."

Dozed. A ceiling. The sky rests, disease of labour begins. Many who labour all their lives for less reward. O yes, the billboard houses its clients, the labour, the labour – there are many such, dozing imperceptibly, expectant and grey. The disease, dis-ease, property, enter the fields of paper, enter and entrance.

The houses are stacks of paper, the people who doze behind smoky glass, who sweat their oak hearts into typewriters, and there is a new slogan, Words Not Things! They are perched at the end of telephones, their intentions strung from hill to hill.

The surfaces begin to jerk along and wrinkle. The surfaces, they are friends, freshener with a pad of cotton, the wool previously squeezed, a face.

A cloud stable behind the billboard. So this is Essex I said, it is surely here, wind and cloud crossing the county, cars move in front of it, slightly.

Sky presses in. Go down and you will find the floor of clouds: a clutch of ink, a gallery of sunlight.

There was shouting in the next room till the novel was finished, pale chapters instead of their minds, pages like disused airfields.

Flesh fades, this encumbrance. The eating is uncontrollable

As you fade, to a hall of silence, at the root of whose dazzle you continue to be eaten and to be. Gaze down on what dazzles, the pattern approaching, coming in fold after fold.

You are amazed by the sea around its own foot, or gathering itself like a lily on the stable billboard, where advertisements still continue to flicker.

What docile steel / a dud lozenge
Appears / among the many irises
Ordinary corn / the picture
Is stretched / before it begins to flake
What air crawls there / sky attacks marble
The water steps into pits and quarries
What repetitious birds / what
Intentions clamour
River of shields / the canvas is
Covered with colours / of earth, earth-colours
Mysterious metals / to paint with
To be painted / the billboard assembled
Is quiet as a hill / vibrating
With the still joy of knowledge / language lies broken
Among the footsteps of things
We are in a watery field
Ghosts of flesh / solid ghosts / ghosts of things
Made abundant

For we have learned to be many, our
Triumph and downfall, flakes off the core;
I can tell you now that from our vantage point
Things have more or less disappeared, there are
No more things, no more of the
Heaps of substance.
Flesh faded, a useless Encumbrance, the currency now is paper.
The blanket swallowed a living bird
At five o'clock, rump of sunlight, outcrop
Shone and was visited by thought. The anxious
Mouth uttered laws, an orange-yellow

Mark came alive, over our smothered names.
Girlish doors over blue gilt ribs were a
Basis for shades to surge up embarrassed.
We could just hear music, peppercorns,
Blind instruments, the core
Becoming apparent, a window's load of trees,
Mind wondering and wandering. The head developed
Tufts at the end of time
Which is talking to itself, a
Stranger in an empty room
A sunless orange. It is
A shudder that we forget.
The wind brings rain, a harbinger.
There are rocks ahead the colour
Of copper, a lake all around us,
Huge consolations of art,
Mountains and all that stuff. Infinity elapses,
The sunlight attacking truth
Its skins are shed, planes
Dozing in the sky.
The garden is a glare of heat, is
Filled with yellow flowers.
There are children splashing in the pool.
She turns off the tap and air remarks
Where else is there to live?

Grieving Signal

1
Sky chill, the water my grimy child
And a great lack of ideas.
I observed our way of keeping quiet

Where all the signs were true. Our grieving signal
 Stuck in a thicket. Someone
Destroyed my story of too many colours.

Pressing the switch marked Ecstasy
The coloured snakes are my friends.
They touch the earth and sleep and listen.

Blue eggs are bits of the sky. The afternoon is too near.

2
Cars wake up for you. I cannot sleep,
Grow loose, the prickle of the flesh.
They're spreading underneath the nail –

Miserable signs. Each village
Is manicured to a turn and resting
Each in its separate vale,

The trees alive with sighs. In dream
We went past the curtain of refusal.
One by one we returned, pale and unsatisfied.

3
I'll tell you a story. Moth flutters
Above the brightening pavement. Listen.
His huge fat body falls.

The traffic blew likewise along our roads.
Fat roses, bits of grit,
An institutional quiet, in which

Our lives are played. The switch of need.
Your breasts sank like two pillows.
Under a grey sky I spun the knife slowly.

Three o'clock news: the beasts are absent
Quartered away from their fields.
Amid a litter of biscuits we are afraid

Each striving for some significance.

4
And in the scheme of duty we return
To noon's refusal, vowels; units of silence.
Once picked, the fennel quickly wilts.

I suck the stalk juice.
Animals' bodies, printed out on roads
(In hundreds round here) hum with peace.

5
Noon's business – herbal units.
A bridge ties the knot, beneath goes
Infernal sluggish glare.

A fractured state, then trees
Hurrying over the plain.
Across the field in waves light travels,

A twinge of blue in the sky.
Chastened by dust, a story
Such as sustained the wrapper, a gauntlet –

You plus me plus her in her
Cot and pen. Each midnight
My anger weds itself to a feast.

Lip Service

Prelude
A morning of grey sky and lorries.
The blood streams. Stock of stored gases.
It is a tonic. It is a gale.

Lip Service
The curtain of appearance is settling into
This sort of perpetual being-here.
A lump of immoveable cloud

Just where the road's verge flaps. Her lip
Trembled. Seen over the car's shoulder
The dense lane is whitened

With cow parsley, what we were driving
Down and into. All evening
A faint light shone, here and there in the sky.

There and Back
Spectator of his own low nothingness
The collector with a hurried eye
Goes out to see the grasses in the wind,

The bitter separation of root from flower.
The cloth-covered provisions
Are safe in any gale. Then homewards.

Down here is impermeable –
'Cleansing milk with extract of cucumber.'
You are distracted. Their car returns.

The afternoon, pale as paper, covers the road.

To Glastonbury
Imagine these 'islands', each in its
Puddle of mist, Jurassic outcrops
Rising up from the marshy plain.

A flaw in the history of stone.
These foolish legends. The careful ruins.
As the world thickens with people

The shrub, heavy with water, is pressed
Against a wall, springs back. Traffic sways
Near. We leave the streets and turn

Up to the Tor in the rain.

Reading and then Thinking
About 2 p.m. the novel peters out
In a shower. The afternoon warms up slightly.
I stepped out onto the terrace.

The heavy wet garden. Leaves
Turning their heads back pale in the wind.
One quick gaze into the future.

The light crosses a lattice of fields
Easing us into the thoughtful-descriptive.
I wash carefully, plunging at the margins

Opening out
In the secret region of breath,
Into all that windowing of the forgotten,

Forgotten.

At Ashen Barrows
You are somebody in the early hours
Secretly crossing a hill, scarcely
There, a shadow on the whitened grass.

As summer rain drummed on the leaves
She leaned forward, putting something into the car.
The wind steered into a hedgerow.

The sun came out again.
It was more politic to wait.
Let the meaning lie in the shadows.

Eight barrows pimpled the hill.
Flies settled on their cowpat plateau.
The wealth of small, elusive, growing things –

Our smiles cracked open by the breeze.

Bleeding Hearts
Purple toadflax, the bleeding beans, the shifting
Clouds, the television, the telephone wires, the campion,
The horse-chestnut, the grass, the peppermill and the road.

Puddles start on the terrace. Plastic chairs.
They'll be back soon. Trees, the remote waiting,
A blackbird pulling something out of a wall.

On the TV a speckled race-track
Where the sunlight slants and falls, like it did here.
A quick cup before they arrive, and a turn

Round the village or up on the hill perhaps.
The pictures are pinned around an empty frame.
Wind blusters in the hollows. The birds get ready

For something more sustained in the way of music
Stationed here and there in the tops of bushes.
Dust speckles the milk. We are all here

And weighted with a bell-like certainty.

Snow in April

Snow in April
   The flakes come so slowly
Out of the depths of the sky – the ones
   Higher up, seeming to float
Parallel to the earth
   Are a flickering screen out of which
These others descend
   Framed by the platform roof,
An endless succession, suspended, all
   Movement transformed into stillness. The tulips

Erect, then bending to the shower

The page worn threadbare with our comings and goings.

Dreams Dreams

How to convey the dictionary home
Across streets of bruised wordage?
A tree like an emptied purse is waiting,

Its stranded arms over concrete. The stanzas
Are strangers, daffodils outside banks
A prompt drug that I am homing on.

Some quiet sex is embossing the bushes,
Bound back and pruned and
Springing forth in flurries.

I salivate money and verses. A fine
Network falls on the paper.
Rain in many pale colours. I drown

In the map, I am flooded with tints,
Sleeping in insults. The two huge books
Rest on my chest as I tell my story:

Cockfosters wept, day declined
Over Bounds Green and Southgate.
The sun went red, then ceased its operations

As I opened the blood-package,
As I returned to my birthplace
The scene of a thousand crimes.

On those whitened mornings, trains
Pulled up out of the distances.
Benches weren't warmed by the sunlight.

Filled with a thought of silence
I rose at an early hour.
I travelled north through suburbs.

I came as slowly as I could
Hand over hand, along the rope of flight
And all the way here I made up stories.

Shunning the insect dazzle, in your pale flight
You'd struggled into bloom, your lips cried open,
Turned inside out, a sunflower.

Stained glass shone bright in each doorway.
Chrysanthemums stood in front gardens
Their bronze flowers slaughtered by the frost –

Emblems of power, each rooted in defeat.
I prepare myself
To put back together the fragments of mourning.

Together we'd come here in secret
With pieces of bark like cloth across our faces.
A flock of pigeons rubbed the winter sky.

Growing terser, the fiction
Was bitten from the apple.
I was this, on the border of its cry:

Uncle, father, grandfather
Conversing with the light-filled rose.
They're in it now, all done for.

I go down the kneeling roads, each human
Is a rift in the wall of cars,
Is a strange gap of blood.

Face, iris, dusk, the wilting fire.
My father's death frees silent places
Filling them up with voices.

Braiding the Squadron

The autumn telephone speaks
Through the flying leaves. I am standing
In yellowing light, holding this something black.
My voice carries, shifting over
The rumpled afternoon, a voice in a cloud.
The tree remembers its head of leaves,
A stripped trunk propping up wires in a
System of dying fields. It remembers
As it hums with a press of conversations.
I press my lonely ear
Pleading for distance, and the aerial roads
That take me nearer and further over
The sagging garden swept clean.
This pattern of conversation takes place
In a thoroughly wet October. The rainwashed cars
Are alert little bodies poised along pavements,
Lawns still fattening, the emptied skies.
There is afternoon rain on the quiet statues
And a huge purpose, hitherto undisclosed.
You have to strive to make a special effect
Because you will die, there are children –
Your notion of the future turning to blood
Somewhere ahead, where stationary boxes reflect
The wind of current events, pieces of sky.
The continuance is another concealed sunrise.
The interest lies in its limits –
Sky written on by clouds, an enthusiastic
Scroll of ocean. I should like to begin
To tell you about it, getting beyond
These intervals of dark. I devour my task
Watching the crystal numbers on my sill
Slowly blacken. My beginning loses itself.
It returns to the end where it started
Soiling the threshold with its bloody arrival.
Another moist sun already rises

Into the surprising sky, there are
Bodies piling up in the hall of mirrors
Reflecting change. The slow vehicle of desire
Like a tractor is crossing the brown field today.
At noon three people paused in the painting
Utterly still, disparate, gazing back,
One diffident, one enquiring and one
Remote in the self-absorbed gaze of childhood.
Those dusts are furled back into their fields.
The authors with one accord observe ahead
Illumination hidden in a cloud.
I rose, put a fist through the picture,
A capsule nursed by water, light and space,
The mothering air. To our lightning
The world is thunder, intelligence shimmers.
Roots of identity, torn up, are
Pale on the surface.
I wait in the terminology bureau.
The gulf of experience is sealed with a smile.
The room is cluttered with voices, conditions.
I am trapped by my consolations. I go to the window.
Why is the four o'clock sunlight so strange . . .
Towards the station now, winter sky will be purple.
Seasons ago leaves here were drinking the light
When I was a child on the huge green lawn,
When I was a boy in the orderly suburb.
In playgrounds children exploded
Summer-long, flower of routine. The milk van purred.
Cherry trees scattered their petals on cars
As if they came from a festival.
And one tree pinkish red, against a
Banked-up sky. We are
Specks of dust in a trough of sunlight.
Summer and winter the gardens open and close
Like fists, and everywhere outside, the

Reefs of air. The efficient day opened
Onto a new sense of failure, more bracing.
Nothing reborn was beating the drum of the air.
We slept in our sheets like bleached flags.
Dawn, the bruised streets as darkness faded.
I looked down onto the pale garden, wondering
The way dark turned to light, like a
Glove turned inside out. I remembered
The first bus changing gear on the hill,
Criminal music of my breathing.
Your face broke the crust of the mirror.
Loads of busy small animals stirred.
Standing among these seasons like doors
Our dreams are the rags of legend,
Days no more than a quiet game of cards
On the solitary cloth, nothing left to hold.
Winter's bud grows, the image shakes off dust.
Houses will swell among the trees of summer,
The lampshade like a sea urchin shine above
Sofas, subdued crowds, the storm
Beyond the threshold, it is now a habitation
Decorated with telephones.
Always such missed connections the city ends in
Tiredness, a swelling of green, the burning
Traveller caught between nowhere and nowhere
And these withdrawn, irascible afternoons,
This trivial rain, its sparkle on grass.

Buddleia

1
Buddleia: the branch
Of musky odour

Seen from the top of a bus
Where it flourished among the rubbish

In the heat tap-tapping
On corrugated iron.

The long and the purple –
Butterflies drowse on its sleeve

Like the scent of an absent name,
Like the life I imagine I have

Summoning me at daybreak, the book
Lying open beside me –

That portrait with the perfect eyes and mouth
Staring intensely back. There is

An oil of light easing the hinges,
A day and a page,

A plain wood box on my desk, containing
Sunflower seeds and fossils.

2
From rape to an impenetrable stillness:
Daybreak over the town,

Slow light with busy winds
As an eye gently opens, sweeping across;

Odd inscrutable flights of birds
Announcing sky. You hold

A piece of the cloth
Of the various clouds and weathers.

Today is a day of warm westerlies,
Rain-bloated blackberries hang,

The bloodstained tissues, remnants of storm,
Scattered by dustmen across the road.

A branch in the garden, lifting, inscribes
On the wall its calligraphy of shadow –

The writing itself is a kind of deafness,
And the flatness of it, a gruff wind, sustained

By cup after cup of the air.
Rain-dashed heads of flowers littered the entrance.

But the suburb is indecipherable
Entered, at an acute angle, suddenly.

3
My head's ablaze with all the absent paintings.
In the butcher's shop there are tongues

Hung up as if to dry
In the faintly smoky morning.

I have a ticket for the art.
The park's a huge green lake of light.

Towerblocks, waterbirds
Dabble the fringes.

Here they come, the attendants
In their dainty uniforms of grey and green.

Blemished by sunshine, the attendants
Have arrived just in time. The landscape

Has been secured, our cars
Fall silent under the trees.

The sunlight's clients in the parks
Are serious, clothed in their solids

And now the drops of morning vanish.
A scent of mock-orange blows through traffic.

In a cool room
The city decomposes into views

The scarce nouns nestle in their frames.
The rape is buried under the city

At the curious junction: us.
Infirm among the colours

We take our refuge
In the helplessness of being a spectator.

Resting on the forgotten strata
Our art is how to survive

Into the next future,
The landscape crackling beyond the mist.

4
Late in the afternoon, a blaze of sun
Perhaps follows the rain.

It dazzles the window.
The house's silence is close as a breath.

Buddleia, the long grey green
Leaves are astream

Beside the exhalations of traffic
As the sky opens out above us,

The sunlight flooding my desk
I take you in my arms

The city roaring all round us.
Thirty or so young men

Being gathered today in our street,
Music shaking the house behind them

In tams and dreadlocks are playing
A noisy game of football.

Bouncing off cars, taunting the drivers.
They deflect the traffic one iota

Then bend before it like the plants.
In my room at the back it is quiet

And I can hear one dove,
From an enormous rift the music rising.

Five Preludes

1
Although you'd like to go down there
And be their witness for an hour,
   (The heat and sunlight finger them)
   Your life begins to thicken and slow.

Old Cream British Sherry
And the carriage is Out of Order.
   Attentively you shrink
   Into the sunlight's pupil,

Look up the embankment's skirt
At whitish nettle-flower
   And the urban sycamore
   Drawn into obstinate leaf,

Lean over, doubly-distanced,
The low railings of your desire.
   A ticketed impermanence,
   You are the closing carriage door

And pause here between flights
Obedient to a fading inscription
   Learning how to float
   One inch above the surface.

Afternoon crowds sigh,
Learning to turn on their root of purpose.
   Each one imagines he slips through
   Into the blue, the only true.

2
Lime trees gathered the heat
From bands of air, and broadcast perfume.
    The memory of our bodies
    Went underground, leaves

Champion the cause. You remember
What comes from the sweet part of you
    Alternately soft and hard –
    That is its supple virtue.

The tunnel of garden, upended,
Concludes in a changing screen of cloud
    On which wide background swifts
    Continually strive.

They scream right up to our house,
Veer off across
    But our pale maps are spread
    Near an impossible border.

Tonight I should like to drink with you
Down by that sleek and tainted river
    Where couples go off into undergrowth
    On the other side, and into

A musky scent of elder
Between the flats and the reservoir
    Down twisting, secret paths
    To seek what's written there.

3
Their mute return. What will you do
With what there is left to be done,
    Who once existed
    With an exiguous grace –

Your appetites are scorned.
Your distances now press
    To the earth in dusty twilight.
    This traffic is a mist.

No rinsing of thirst with solace
But this unholy frieze, a screen
    On which the creatures strive
    For survival. You pass the battered

Milestone's face and racing clouds
Reflected in a still canal.
    Like mercenaries these monuments
    Grow closer round your heart.

Industrial decline –
Its huge and desolate machines.
    The seeding rose bay willowherb
    Along the embankment's a cloud of silver.

You are read as a faint brand of light
At the checkout point. O the brilliant
    Packaging, and the shabby
    People who shuffle past.

4
Or else, deep into the wild
Garden of my days
    I sink to another mode,
    Forgetful of myself.

I walk home, the afternoon
Is hollowed out like a stalk.
    The orange rose is huge.
    It flourishes in carbon monoxide

Along a fraying edge
Of garden, lying between
    Curtain and lorry –
    A threadbare, swaying defence.

The girl at the till's far from water.
Her fingers chatter where numbers flow.
    Mid-afternoon, the city
    A slow-moving parade of signs.

Somebody sick for home
Has planted a vine, broad-leaved as memory.
    The police are parked outside.
    The radio crackles, attentive, all-hearing.

Your words are the flicker of leaves
On a curving surface of noise;
    It is written to a measure
    Slowly becoming known.

5
Magnificent sky of late afternoon
And the lamb quartered for our domestic pleasure
    Arrives with a scroll,
        A thawed papyrus of sacrifice –

The price stained with the blood
Which goes in among the other rubbish,
    Which came to you
        And all the way. It draws you in.

Now here is the poem of me
That is made for you as night falls,
    Dusk-chatterer. From the lettered
    Earth who breathes and arises.

DUST SETTLED

The Explosion

They will smooth your hair
Enquiring politely after your health –
There's a sense of conspiracy
Here in the garden

Where it happened and only quite recently.
No one's saying. It's a beautiful
Garden and people recover
By ignoring the quiet corpses.

How are you? Have another. What's his?
All the time it's getting harder to locate.
There are one or two who want to do something.
By now the corpses have gone.

The flowers smell wrong and the people are beautiful.
Smoothing and stroking one another's hair
They look as if they have just left a film-set
But still it's going on

Somewhere, the echo of that explanation.

Downshire Arms. Hampstead 1971

National Curriculum
As issued by the Department

English Level 2: Writing
Separate ideas / sentences should be identified. At least two of these should begin with a capital letter and end with a full stop.

The writing must be chronological. There must be more than one character, one event and an opening.

English Level 3: Writing
The pupil must write independently with recognisable sentences – more than half of which must be correctly punctuated.

The writing must be chronological and have at least three different sentence connectives or phrases used to relate events i.e. next; so; because; although; first of all; soon after . . .

The writing must have more than one character, one event and an opening, a description of setting or feelings or motives of characters; and a defined ending or a dialogue.

English Level 4: Writing
Stories should have an opening, a setting and more than one character; a series of events and an ending. There should also be evidence of at least two subordinate clauses or expanded noun phrases eg:

Subordinate clauses: 'The family, WHICH was rich and powerful, broke the law, KNOWING they would not suffer' (the use of 'which' and 'knowing'.)

Expanded noun phrases: 'the below-store car park'; 'shining new lace-up shoes'; 'dark green leaves changing to a lighter green at the edges'; 'a cold blustery / windy day' or 'a cold January day.'

Lucy, Cheryl and Charles

Harriet shut two expensive windows silently. "Come here". She wondered. The dog held on. They entered the elegant tree carefully. "Go away" he requested. Lucy aged. Charles left the small river easily. "Yes please" he echoed. He sank back. Lucy called. Some dead chairs quickly. "No thank you" she replied. Charles sang. The cat crawled over a handsome table kindly. "Good evening" he answered. Cheryl laughed. Cheryl swam some smelly gardens quietly. "How are you?" she asked. Henry wept. A bird destroyed one cheap house noisily. "What's the time?" it asked. It died. Jim opened a large door clumsily. "Where?" he stated. They reached out. You opened the unusual drink grimly. "When?" he wondered. The dog held on.

"The day before yesterday, Lucy" the cat retorted beautifully. She will go over his face gradually. The day after tomorrow the table had killed the fish. Calmly they will move on the table whereas when his hands will move over the desk. Awkwardly he went into the garden after some delay. Supposing the dog had walked over Tony eloquently. It went out of the room. Sometimes it makes my flesh creep. And if reality had shaded his eyes. Cautiously you will run upstairs, frequently. Her hair slowly. He walked out of the air in autumn, because the chairman will sweep Cheryl openly. She will go over his face always. Where her hands jumped beautifully she will move across the garden after some delay. Well. His hands had shaded the floor cautiously. He had gone over her spine sometimes.

She rose to greet the sky. She was lying abandoned in a room. It was light then dark. The bulb boomed.

She laid down another pair of finished wings on the desk by her side and thought about Charles sitting behind his leather-topped one at Over Cray.

She had once remarked that he was like Tony over feeling ashamed.

Occasionally the door would open with a stiffish wedge of air and Lucy could hear Simon's gurgle and Charles' low guffaw.

Simone was sitting up in bed looking about the same age as Tony and Harriet and enveloped in a huge wool nightie that had belonged to Cheryl.

Simon had persuaded James to help him mount her masterpiece so that it was easily transportable on the small wooden platform that would serve as a stage.

Lucy knew that Simone was also giving a hand in an adjoining room.

Lucy hesitated next to wheatfields. Charles waited in front of brickfields. Cheryl sang. Within windows the car stood, before two tables. A bird drifted next to wheatfields. Some clouds passed in front of brickfields. Lucy hesitated within windows. Cheryl sang before two tables. Some clouds were drifting alongside sunlit pools.

"How are you getting destroyed?" one cheap bird asked.

Cheryl's cottage was a small erection dozing among trees. The house was a rough construction laughing among houses. The church was dilapidated, a statue set among magnificent woodlands. The old mill was a thirties building drowsing among its shrubby borders. The factory was a well-tended erection hidden among the houses. A sleek construction dozing among ruins, Cheryl's cottage was remarkable set among its magnificent pines. The house was a tall building set among shrubby borders. Cheryl's cottage was a sleek one set among trees.

Charles' temper, louder than usual, was like Harriet's. A voice, Harriet's voice, louder than usual, was like Tony's driving Lucy's. A hand, softer than usual, was like a complete change. Cheryl's hair, more delectable than usual, was like nothing. Tony's driving, sharper than usual, was like the wind, Charles' love-making, more ill-tempered than usual. It was like a stone. Harriet's sunny mood, louder than usual, was like Lucy's hair, Lucy's temper. Harder than usual it was like a grain of hope. Cheryl's voice, softer than usual, was like a block of ice.

"Where have you been?" he whispered. Cheryl coiled among flashing meadows. "Why has he stopped?" she pleaded. The path wound through wheatfields. "Where has he waited?" Lucy screamed. The road wandered between houses. Harriet rested among the vines. "Why have you waited?" Cheryl shouted. The highway made its way beneath factories. "Where have you stopped?" Charles requested. Time travelled brickfields. "Why has he been?" Harriet retorted. There was a brief silence. Lucy coiled through well-tended gardens. "Where have you been?" he shouted. "Why have you stopped?" she rejoindered. "Where have you seen?" Lucy demanded. Harriet wound between flashing windows. "Who has he asked?" Cheryl asked. Charles wandered along beside rivers of every description. "Where has he struck?" Charles whispered. The river made its way along beside banks of earth. "Why have you seen?" Cheryl whispered.

Cheryl placed her hand on Charles'. The door opened. Charles placed his hand on Cheryl's. She placed Charles' hand on his. His mouth opened. He placed her hand on Cheryl's. She placed his hand on hers. She placed her hand on hers. Her heart opened. Cheryl placed his hand on hers. Charles placed her hand on hers. He placed his hand on hers. The door opened. She placed her hand on his.

Hands atop a desk or cast. Then there was the matter of the silver horse. This had been a gift from Tony, and Cheryl remembered seeing it in the old library at Over Cray. It was a small erection, probably plated, dating from the middle of the last century, and Charles had one wherever he happened to be staying. It wasn't that he needed a carriage clock in every room – he just liked them, that was all. The brass frame was certainly handsome reflected Cheryl as she looked at herself in the mirror. "Probably plated" Charles replied. But that had been so long ago, and now that they were together again, time didn't seem to matter. She ran her fingers reflectively over the creature's glistening flanks. Time, memory, these were enigmas. She watched the magnificent creature galloping away over the fields.

The rivers were distributed according to some principle of symmetry such as Charles.

He entered the tree and its trunk closed round him with all the finality.

The river, the fields held all his attention, and it was as much as Cheryl could do to.

Finally they reached a place of magnificent dreams. Finally they reached a place of strange and opulent dreams. Finally they reached a place of fruitless and exotic dreams. Finally they came to a place of dreams. Finally they came to a place inhabited exclusively by dreams. Here there were dreams, leaving a deposit on the glass. The dreams flitted about the air like shadows. On all sides you could see nothing but shadows. The air was full of cool, blunt shadows. The area was crowded with elusive grey shadows. One shadow pushed across a window, and a whole class of shadows stood around the house at noon. These particular shadows were crisp as silhouettes and quite motionless. Then Cheryl remembered seeing it all. The room began to grow cold. The shadows disappeared behind a mirror. "Of such was the orient glare of dawn". The mirror hung like a cold fruit. He was able to give it his undivided attention. It hung like a cold sun, like a portrait. It hung on all sides. The shadows had all gone into the mirror. It was a small shaving mirror. It was an intelligent mirror. It was a small large mirror. By now the storyteller was completely cold. Lucy and Cheryl and Charles were gazing into the long mirror of the past. Trees were lying there being their own fruit. Lucy and Cheryl and Charles lay there like trees. The storyteller had disappeared. There was no on at all left to cry.

And Ada Ann

The skin trunk was absolutely empty, but the inside of the lid of it was lined with sheets of what I now know to have been a sensational novel. It was of course a fragment, but I read it, kneeling on the bare floor, with indescribable rapture. It will be recollected that the idea of fiction, of a deliberately invented story, had been kept from me with entire success. I therefore implicitly believed the tale in the lid of the trunk to be a true account of the sorrows of a lady of title, who had to flee the country, and who was pursued into foreign lands by enemies bent upon her ruin . . . The fragment filled me with delicious fears; I fancied that my mother, who was out so much, might be threatened by dangers of the same sort; and the fact that the narrative came abruptly to an end in the middle of one of its most thrilling sentences, wound me up almost to a disorder of wonder and romance.
        'Father and Son' by Edmund Gosse

The great thing about this author is that he never makes anything up.
        Reviewer discussing a novel by Len Deighton

The Novel
A closed day, the well-tended clouds
Were squadroned behind the rooftops.
Getting up Dick heard
The friendly sound of the Novel downstairs.
He called up Ann. He heard
A sort of buzz, he saw
A foam of black on white.
Across the carpet it fell
Opening deferentially
In slices – like chapters Dick said.
Outside the clouds detached themselves,
Weather touching the building, a marriage.
Dick was hiding
In the telephone's corridors,
His voice brushing the rooftops.

Afternoon
Talking about the planes
Fills up the sky. A single bulb
Burns in the ceiling.

Under the afternoon's blanket
Roads twitch, a mother gently
Watches her daughter growing up.
There is always something to look at.

Five o'clock.
Ann is coming in over the fields. Ann.

Poem
Draw back from a cooling body.
Don't let him see you. Never say you.
One week to an opening. Shhh!
Traffic goes overhead.
The distances, Carol, your drawing on the table.
She grows up patterned in light
Anointing his anger. Oceans begin to build
And a mother holds fast to her daughter,
Their shadowy claims
Stretching around the globe.

Him and Ann
Whatever made you do such a thing
Ann? He sat on the edge.
A sofa waited. There were
Some showers about, and on the edge
Of one a rainbow glinted.
    The radio said
"This is coming from Highway Thirteen".
Problem: the choice of a body
From which one can elicit
The right cries, presumably.

Presumably, said Ann
Whose stomach turned over a little.

She watched
Her fingernails for hours.
"Whatever made you?"
At that she almost...

Ann, Her Life and the Room
She was reading the map of his hands
Fastened to the window, refer to the table.
The picture was also crooked.

When he was doing something
Usual, like cleaning a mirror, it
Would suddenly start, her mother's example
Like the day she was named
After a tomb. That hand had been in the family
For five generations.

Outside they are repairing the termitary
    Ann is alone and listening to the sound
That other people's lives make.
The room, Ann, she is crossing a floor.
She is all around it, its signature.
The way his feet rest on the ground.
The desk, roads and dreams.

Ann and Cynthia. She was used to
Keeping them under the bed,
Along the windowsill in rows
Then she looked at his head beside her,
The way it breathed easily.

Sex is the furniture,
Is filling a bowl of flowers.
Ann, the adapted room –
"Write it here on my hand" she was saying
As she cradled his head
All through the winter.

He is drinking the ocean beside her bed
Walking around a shadow,
Someone quietly issuing orders,
Waking at five,
Letting this one fall and that one rise
In a pillar of smoke.

His walls are covered with maps.
The bed was rumpled strata.
Aspirin.

Ann on Her Way to Work
Fog covered the north
All morning. She was
Using it as a yardstick
Dreaming of dawn berries
Clustered in the fridge,
A cloud of former bloom
Filling up shrivelled gardens.

She shifted her back in the bath
While trees faded, loosening
Mist into the air.
She dreamed she was in the lift
Upright and silent –
Generations
Were crowded in the basement

And so to move
Crabwise over the city
Past its mysterious barricades.
Ann had a worrying day.
The boss wasn't there
And the office lift stuck.
She waited in her shoes.

Home again Ann crossed a window
But stronger than a shadow,
Tarnished,
Her meal cooled past all reckoning.
"Give me a voice – no, one like yours."
He silently appeared
Settling overhead like a rocket.

Ann Setting Out
"Falsity, my blood is false
Seen through the shell of a window
Where they are sitting on their knees
Braiding hair

He saved her from the other side
Of paradise with his plans –
The way his face breathed sincerity
In the underground.

Now Ann is crossing the city
Getting bigger, her feet
Walking over the ground,
This watching music, already
The distances, beginning to be heard

And Ann was grateful, sailing easily
Over the floor she travelled
Every day on the tube for thirty
Years, the same pair of black gloves.

White Eggs: A Coda
The mind away, it's exciting. Good wing mirrors essential. Eggs, wing are the mind. Its good essential. Are wings? Eggs, attractions at beavers. Essential mirrors good, exciting. It's away, the mind.

The mind beavers away, its attraction exciting. Good wing mirrors essential. Beavers away at attraction's exciting eggs. Wing mirrors are the mind. Away at its exciting eggs, good wing mirrors are essential. Beavers at its attractions. Eggs, good wing, are essential. The mind away, its attractions exciting. Good wing mirrors essential the mind beavers at. Exciting eggs good. Mirrors are essential. Beavers away at attractions. Eggs, good wing are essential. The mind away at its exciting good. Wing mirrors essential. The mind beavers at its attractions. Eggs.

The mind exciting – good. Beavers, eggs. Wing mirror away, mirrors at, are its essential attractions.

The mind essential. Beavers are away. Mirror at wing. It's good. Attraction. Eggs, exciting eggs. Attraction's good. Its wing at mirrors. Away are beavers. Essential the mind.

Helen and John

She listens or lies in a coma. Political dreams
Like frozen food litter the driveway,
Each morning that struggle for breath – the plot unfolds.
Part one's engraved on glass.
All fiction echoes the apocalypse
(That first big bang), the sun comes up
Over the rooftops saying that you're alive.
His wasn't the name of a famous painter
His mistress interjects, in red
Meanwhile the days all concertina outward.
He marvels at his own egotism,
Puts on a shirt to
Start, with borrowed laughter

Helen woke up with a plan
For walking the city and watching
Its baked down cries, to finish
When the moon rises.
                        Before midday arrives
Her portrait will be done in pastel.
A medical friend shines the eyes.
She borrows a helpful mirror.
Visiting the doctor
John points at a picture of himself.
'This is where it hurts.' Insects
Are starting to hibernate in curtains.
Small explosions dot the city.
The mass of air divides.

'Life is a Dream' – he wrote this down
Before she looked away
Then went upstairs to what he called
His special silence. A sagging sofa
In the Hotel Temporary where lives
Pass in a blur, are shaded by routine.
Outside the blossom flows like traffic
Transgressing a border of trees.
She's taking her lover's story from a drawer.
'The rift is where they went, those men of air
Taken away from here, bleached
Characters. Helplessly they strove
For some significance.' She wakes up listening
For his departure. Blood
Throbs round her heart in that silence.

"You, folding a cloth or sitting at work"
Bending and rising. Off you go
Harvesting plants that spill out oxygen.
Between the river and the mountain
Lives a population of a million souls
Striped with roads and bleeding smoke.
Fictions for ever beyond your reach
Subside into the distance, watercolours
On a damp page of sky
And in the room you almost call yourself
She settles, among the cushions. There is
A constant monotonous note
This something that pre-vents
The answer's footfall. Coming soon.

He'll be here soon, the artist of the age
With private cries of suffering
That we can do nothing about.
Hollowed out of the wind's side
Is a tree that bent to listen once.
The title of the picture's 'Orpheus
Killed by Sobbing Maenads', the day
So still a shadow halfway up the tower block
Seems it will never move. "Is everything
I tried to write unrecognisable?
The more I add the more I take away."
It's time to glory in the pretence.
As day by day the colours deepen
He listens for their soft return.

Haggard with sleep she wakes to snow –
A pact coating the eyes with silence.
Is he still there examining the jaws
That chew through paper? The hours turn black.
She points to a picture, villa on a hill.
"This is the story you can enter
Anywhere you like." The words
Summon it up – somewhere between
Feeling and intellect it sheds
Light back on them, the way they start to live
In rooms they'll call themselves
Where, sunlight entering the carpet,
The pattern that they strove for starts to fade.

The Brood of Fiction

As in a dream to the bearded household parent pretending to be wise, the maternal indifferent focus, to the ghosts and doctors: we all advanced to the same position slowly.

Dedication
Water inherits my thirst
The raindrops people a bush
That's solid with wintry shadow.

Millions of days have visited here
Around the eye's shuttered case
In rooms where the sunlight droops

And a parting of the sentinel leaves –
Here and there there are voices
The night spoons me various bodies.

The Fiction
Stripped trees plunge in the streetlamps.
Mysteries of the tarot. A girl
Plays with incense in her room
That overlooks the square. Night-breath
Pressing on curtains and mysteries of increase.
The memory potion is distilled in a spoon
And their dusty voices: 'Blood ties must be renewed.'

On the Morning of the First Day
A knocking in the radiator's
Chilled throat then renewal of silence

A tree rains its moments
Onto earth's mirror

Or the steady roar of a fire,
Fire in the bedroom, a homage to illness.

The Images
In the ox's eye
Descartes discovered sight
Cutting a little window
In the back of the eye
He blocked it with paper
And onto this the world fell
Infinitely small, reversed image –
It was like peering into a room,
Is images kissing the light.

Much Later
Tussocky grass melts upright after the frost
By the railway line, the whole thing
Was laid out to be described –
'And when they were away in Arosa
Among the oleanders
I felt that the sentence was death'

Hoarded fragments. Today
I walked past a radiogram on the pavement.
The classics boomed out of a cupboard –
I examined the pillared veneer, the gold
Engraving of sunlight on the wood.
Permanent morning endless day
And the bandaged statues have no option.
We are ghosts of performance.
Being paid to have their opinions
The critics surround us
Voluble like the traffic
And waiting for a bus this sunlit morning

The mirror like light's continuum
I need a fortress to explain
Art, in my shoes
The sky going right down to my feet, a horizon
So comfortable here with its clouds.

The Visit
Walking up from the station, along a path overlooking The Broadway – there are parked cars massed below, a glare of sunlight on their roofs; in polished silence they await the evening migration. Ann in her suburb now, and a branch perhaps that broke open in the space that's between us, explosion of cherry over tended gardens. But when you arrive there'll be no one. Entering like a thief, the Radio Times resting on an embroidered chair. Sunlight on gleaming woodwork, daffodils glimpsed through French windows bobbing about in a breeze that's inaudible in here. Turning aside from the mirror that hangs in the hall, and on out again, like an infection as it roars and fills.

Ann and her husband
Being joined all day
By an axis of silence
On the polished floor of quiet –
He returns down arterial roads.
He buys an evening paper
As badge, as promise.
The newsprint smells of event
And then this
Spillage into sunset, a suburb
Enfolds him, a garden
That swallows him up like a flowery tongue.
So what has she become –

Reversal of all hope
An abstract of desire?
Lets take the Underground

Its loops its curlicues
A single sign
Like lines along your hands.
Potential journeys

Will heal the breach
In understanding:
'Ann is many people
But ultimately me'

As he said one morning walking along
A street of abandoned housewives –
Her body it is a fiction
'What peculiar weather'
Its wrinkled seam, 'I can
Hardly touch you' he said,
'The surface of your story
It wrinkles a surface of milk
Left standing in the pan
                 Code of desire
Smelt here, always renewing remembering
A distillation of crudest energies
Rooms, then journeys

A thoughtful stare at our globe, before
Departure
        Erect and slow
In a coma of desire
A hidden glow of thought, and then
A totally new kind of narrative
Like a field dotted with bushes
As bits of you edge into light
Still rather wary
                Clouds though.

In libraries the afternoon
Sighs, only the books

Seem breathing as pages
Turn themselves each after each

Today Ann is choosing
The book of herself –

S/he is one star
Of the energy that rises

Having entered then left the spectrum
A woman. She catalogues deceit

Is hungry for light where
Someone's mind raids her

Somewhere else she is human, all else
Is passion, expires in

The brain of the novelist
Spectre awakened in surmise

When at five o'clock this androgyne
Arises out of blank water to question me

i.m. *Ada Ann*
First light over caesura –
I woke up at four to write

In my dawn-eyrie, Ann
By the gate, wind in her dress,

The abandoned chapters. A
Specious form of detachment

Is born of hurt and wanting.
She is swallowed up in my mirror

Gasping for breath, Ann in the mind
A theme cheerfully whistled behind the laurel

While I have a new notebook
The sunlight falls on its pages

Gloved hands held a ticket
Wasted beyond recall

Surcease of traffic
A presence on stairs

And I'm lying here your feet
Walking all round me –

Come closer and we shall emerge
In the mirror of our healed selves

Coda
Lonely as clouds, the people
Seize on the street to cover their nakedness
The secrecy of their lives invokes desire –
Rex as Ann, Ann as Wendy, Wendy discovered
By his or her father. "There's something
About how she walks that isn't quite female".
The cinema, ankle-deep in birth wrappings,
Is where fiction gets buttered with fact. It is like
A great blowsy lion fed with flies of stillness.

The Bush of Growth

We grow, we are moving along, the sky mother
Launches her satellites, the face darkens at interphase.
A hand like a cloud is crossing it and a loop
Of growth is spun out in a long thread without breaking.
This animal cloth is always being woven intact.
We hide and we ride, counting the years ahead.

A tusk toots, we look to the years ahead.
The ear sound like an ear affixed to the mother
Who eats what she swallows. The plants remain intact.
A separated head drifts off at interphase.
There is conscious imitation, cells formed by breaking.
The basal body's ear ends in a loop.

A fully denatured strand, double circle or loop
Is thrown out over the growth that starts up ahead.
Foliate systems flourish, a strand is breaking.
Ribs form a basis, slipping away from the mother
Who is new as opposed to old, suspended at interphase.
Range in dry mass, the body remains intact.

The mammal and plant systems remain intact.
There is bunching together, a self-aggregation or loop,
Sage growing on the horizon to flower at interphase.
Birds twitter, offices rise, moving ahead.
It grows at the same end of the original mother –
Agile timber, this ear, this denatured breaking.

Seeds hulled, pods in the sky like clouds are breaking.
Fingered spring the water, water intact
Is whitish. The L shape is typical of a mother
Who multiplies looped circles hiding herself in each loop
The ribs shine out, a basis in years ahead,
A yard of sunlight, a bush of growth at interphase

Filling the sky-roofed dome as it darkens at interphase,
Its active site occupied. The cells formed by breaking
Flood. A range in dry mass rears up some way ahead –
Horizon rock. Horizon appears intact.
By imitation the body has formed a loop
Joined to the same end of the original mother.

Clocks change at interphase, the hands remain intact.
They swing round to avoid breaking in a huge loop.
The years fill up ahead, the sage bush grows O mother.

Again Again

He got up again, force being feedback.
The room was stored energy. What is it? wind
Flowed, his trajectory stuck, there were
Well-defined pathways, the decrement.

He got up again, the floor
Of any physical system, he
Couldn't get up.

A door opened the wind, a
Closed ring or loop of dependencies.
What is it? The structure's
Resonant frequency
Calls forth a force opposing this error.

Wind went over a floor.
He couldn't get up, and amplitude
Increased.
Dimensionless equations of motion
Came between her and the wind.

Bridges flowed, stored energy.
A mechanical load passed over
Comprising inertia and friction.
He couldn't get up.
A closed door opened letting in wind,
Lettered points on the error waveform.
      He tried to get in, he came
In, the dynamic behaviour
Of any physical system
Is
  A torque-controlled motor
  Well-defined feedback pathways
  A closed ring or loop of dependencies
  Oscillations
        Decrement

Later heading off into
Waveforms of dimensionless error.

Diurnal

1
Reflections like marquetry inlaid in a table,
Stay round all afternoon.
The drier's spindle mourns.
Under the sky is a desk, its supports
Like a pair of carved wings. It travels alone
And its wake fills with a buzz
Of our conversations. The wings
Dive underground now – upright and full
I can topple back into myself.
Wings carefully folded I'll sleep.
Next day again their wash ruffles the tops
Of the summer trees – I'm so thankful
To all those people down there
Who are striving so hard to entertain me.

2
So the powers-that-would-be are arranging
Their limbs, round the pool in the park.
As if leaving a dream
I find my way to this picture in the heat,
Sit down awkwardly here at the edge.
The language is there, like a subdued
Household filtering in,
The meaning sensed somewhere behind it.
But today I shrink from beginning.
Such dumbness is the most interesting instrument,
It confronts the flare, darkness then pallor
As a garment's withdrawn, the secret places,
Most interesting folds I can enter.
It's later still, I'm practising out in that vacancy.

3
If only I could, forgetting myself, be simply
This body cutting up meat –
A knife easing its way searches out
The invisible junction between here and not.
But the sky outside being replaced with writing
I am alone here with the mark of myself.
It is something between a fingerprint and a sign
As I climb these unresisting stairs
To look down from an upstairs window
My ageing a process of sunlight while over
The cluttered gardens a hammerhead of cloud
Gathers itself, day's wave
Looming up at me, and a dog
Rubs its voice on the powerful surface of air.

4
It's as if she is climbing
A mountain, racquet in hand, but the other
Is nimble, playing round her feet.
She is a sweating statue, wasting
Helplessly into the past, while the other
Prances over the court's worn table.
She bangs the ball into the net
As the new one sails into harbour.
The Mexicans played a ball-game like this
To mirror the movement of planets. Spectators
Peopled the sad spaces between
Climbing down past the rows of skulls
And over a framework of stars
Immoveable in their courses.

5
In the ear of a cave we had sheltered from wind.
Rocks were dark against sunlit water,
A diagonal river thick-set with alders,
Its leaves voices in a dry classroom
And then a submarine echo returned
Over the floor of water, across the walled fields.
A cliff path swayed, between here and nowhere,
The rocks pastel grey now and playing with scale.
The sea grew somnolent
Around green boulders, it swung like a pendulum
Speckled with sunlight, a respectable postcard.
Reading, we have stayed in the cave
Ageing around the eyes – this is
Partly the sun and the wind.

6
What matters is narrative push, I keep
Telling myself, to keep moving.
We descend to the grubby harbour from our
Bedroom in a tower.
A river slides over slate, our feet
Scrunch shingle and stinking weed,
The stain of growth, fur of lichens.
Me, I collect the world.
I place salt on my tongue, from the
Salt box as a reminder
Watching the river fade away among stones.
World drinks the world.
Under its foot of departure I groan.
(So far it keeps me from reaching you.)

7
Rain grazes the sea's surface, clouds are like
Cattle the wind herds past the last islands,
Past gulls in their rainy cities.
Then a bright patch arrives between them
And the pool is like a Victorian greetings card.
There is primrose and polythene among the burnt gorse.
There's a lark perched on a bank
Where the vernal squill's in flower, and still
Behind me this murmuring, the ocean
Turns   in its bed   as far as
Where the rocks' hazardous tumblings stop.
Structures of rage: I have balanced
So long on the outside here, looking
Down to the darker ocean in your eye.

8
"Well here we are installed in a tower.
We haven't had a dud cup of tea
In Wales and on a clear day from here
You can see Weston-super-Mare easily."
Sections, to weave in and out of, skylark,
Observations, the Warpool
Conversations in the hotel
Prussian blue was the waves' colour
That morning, came rolling in with their eyes.
The little silky ones lapped
While geologists tapped with their hammers
"Shirley looked tiny against the cliff face –
She saw a bird up there, was it a stonechat."
A slatey sea glared between ruggerposts.

9
As if by accident these stones dropped
All over the headland. Here they made fields
And out on their loaf-shaped island
Fed on the young of gulls. They lit
Fire on stone, brought the sun down
Where serpents coiled
And coins fell. Hush. Grain, lice
Some fire as purifier. Who killed
The indigenes and peopled emptiness,
Feet creaking on the stairs? We saw
A beehive sunning itself by a wood
Our parents in the church, then wheat
In sheaves, our childhood holidays. The postcards
Were shards of memory, fallen stones and grain.

10
Hanging out here
In Autumn city air
Wearing a curvy smile –

On escalator, riding down
Time: ten twenty three, slides overhead
Then down under the city

Racing on and into the grate
Past seasons'
Smile and frown, I've been away

So let's swap pronouns
Anchored to each rusty root
I feel I fail –
Corrupt our cave, this city
That hurries, moves us through its ground.

11
And tomorrow being such another, the top of a column
Becomes visible now, like a bird table, pigeons
Gathering, sparrows. Tomorrow
We are new in our clean clothes.
I'll also be travelling the city's impermeable
Timetables, a grid laid over it, phonecalls
Tomorrow renewing the house's corners.
But tonight cars sigh in a broad river, nothing
Stops them, not even this banked heat.
Disturbances in the upper atmosphere
Hint at it, earth rolls steadily onward
Till night departs, like a man putting on his coat,
And my body spreads out white as dawn
Under those listening trees.

12
How the day should be at its beginning –
Much was due to the fury of that conquest.
It is a story telling itself,
A tongue questing in an ever open mouth.
A man at a typewriter wanted to begin.
He said, "Day rises at my calling –
A still cloud waiting to be told.
I'll stand on the edge of you describing it
While buildings go past in procession,
Word-eaten sorrows and songs.
A fly crawls to the edge of my page.
A sponge being removed from ocean,
It swells again, as I pass under archways
With bits of information adhering."

13
He died on the vibrating table
For the second time one April noon.
The sun glared briefly, flowers
Bequeathed their sundry heads
Whose colours will shrink back into the seed.
Hushed traffic bore him away, outside
We swayed on the pavement like trees
Adjusting our little fences.
Rain came then sun the rain that fingered
British hillsides. Under ceilings
Our bodies were precise as clocks.
Time was a fever, behind oak-coloured
Glass our bodies in a sweat.
At one o'clock we unwrapped lunch.

14
The first chapter, he said.
She agreed with that. Abundance.
Together they couldn't help making something.
It was all they could manage.
Upstairs the children's voices strove.
Her name was Marjorie. He was called Jack.
Off you would go, she had said
Into the mists of day. He agreed.
It was a conundrum. Vaguely her voice
Rose and fell silent again in a column.
Sleep was a monument to them both.
Especially in broad daylight – two sacks
Of breath, two pairs of nostrils.
Her hands fought something off, was it marriage?

15
The sun was wheeled out into the sky
Like a respectable crook. It shone.
Her taut tides were what he imagined then
Prolonging tedium, delicious dream,
The lawn of afternoon swabbed down
By greyish cloud. A bud, a stride –
"Hop in" she said. They drove to the sea.
Beside the garden gate, thighs wide, she
Came in the sun, light spattered
Her body, and later this other hand
Was stroking the grain of his suit, respectable
Crooks who enjoyed the cool of the evening
Each plucking their fruit from the tree,
Conspiring together to call it marriage.

16
They flounce   he goes   open to argue
The memorable desk
Throat hung with veins

Birdlists: warblers
Avocets / charity
There are grebes on the reservoir

Like a grey shoe the lake
Was dimpled   Surly doors

A memorable throat
Desk of illusions
Typewriter magnificence a type of howl

Needs somewhere all the same
To lay its small hard head

17
Open black door to gape
Grey dawn's a rusty hinge
The unknown future comes

So tried another morning
Tasted it, tested it like a teething ring
From bed came forth saw clouds
And trees being busy
Offices. Bored with anger even,
He found he loved the glare
Walking uphill and wanted to be eaten.

Now like the sea
He ripples gently to his target –
The port of her, the slowly swelling
Port of her.

18
Breathed in, then out, there's wheat among the cushions,
Its ticklish presence. He's a
Glacier of rib. Gate clangs.
Shirt of woven fire, tie of regret
And these occasions stir
Other eventful memories – his belt
A curved snake saved from a childhood garden.
Corpsed on the shining lino their grievance
Is shared while waiting for a phone or guests.
The iceberg furs, such calculations,
A granite ink just right to kindle meat.
Thighs and hurrying Autumn clouds
Are what he likes to remember, doorways
Filling with darkness to balance on future wind.

19
The nude, such vivid integument, body
Joined by its gristle. The ropes of
Sinew were tying him down.
Before the mirror he rose in a thought
Of himself, was vainly seeking himself
In a heap of clothes, this
Whispering shell becoming
A sky. Birds held in its corners,
Dispossessed, pecked at the veil
Which was now a hardened curtain painted with fruit.
Running he found the sea.
A dignified remnant he ran
Beside kitchen-slabs of water, alongside
The waves' bobbing motion.

20
Music on the sea a storm of sound,
His fingernail moons a displacement of years.
A voice paused at the door, smell of
Home, smell of destinations, a tongue
Reaching for words. He gave
A disenchanted snort, then remembered
Berries, childhood, a wall again
Was clamouring in the heat. "Our lives
Are a novel being read by somebody else –
We make it sound like poetry." He looked
Into the face of his feelings and couldn't see.
The noise of possessions is lost in a clock
Where, on a coast between land and water,
The unknown millionaire dies.

21
Something to better my surfaces – I am
Over you, like a cloud.
My face growing dark is descending
Into your trade of waves. The past
Overtakes the present, it topples.
Metal tongues flutter.
All round the edge they invade us
With a grinning sense of forlorn.
The wind gets up, sea is serious
Beyond us. It whitens the carpet.
Edge-furls. There is a rustle
Of You turning the pages
In this quiet room where we store
Our bodies like so many fictions.

22
Earthrise, and you go gently forward.
The friendly planets lie down.
Leaning over you, I was
Growing accustomed to that pose
Fruit ripening on its branch, our language
Breathed jointly onto glass. Who
Named us, head and its shadow
Afloat on the wall? We hid from the sky,
Dipped a finger in the secret,
Placing it to our lips. Each wrote
On a windowpane steamy with morning
While contraries talked, drowning in the wide bed.
There is no end to this writing letters
Each to each from opposite planets.

23
In trees dark with noon birds fell quiet –
Why so dark? Is it us in the future?
Slowly I turn in the act in a spiral.
Day's shutter opens then closes.
Now here is the famous weather,
A wish to be with the flesh –
Wind in our voices, and beginnings of rain.
Rain broods on the motherly mountain
We have come to a whispering place, at the
Head of the rails. A torn curtain flaps.
Clouds are peeled back to reveal the sun.
The days are arches following arches.
We sit tongue-tied through another evening.

24
The one door swung between two doorways
And both were equally dark
And mysterious. Now I am living
Among my books and we both shelter there
Under the window's lid.
Trees on the road outside
Are annually lopped. This morning
One was cut down and carted away.
The bright stump remains. Some flowers
She bought me have almost died.
Darkness crowns both our heads
Coming down like soot onto the sill.
It will strike at our one root –
The absurd fiction that something was owned.

25
With their eyes hungering for oblivion,
Metal of green ones, a chink of green metal
They surround a chair, their necks swaying

Or hiding inside oblivion's beard, their
Fantasies fizz, sunrise –
One two three four five

Or bent in a corner, in a supper of shadows
Eyes searching you our
Among the clergy.

Wind ruffles the students' heads.
Your life is not yours, it belongs to another,
The hero of the sculpted hair.

Remember the boring films you went to?
Now tower equals mist where secretaries take hold.

26
A station nameplate creaks in the wind.
All together we rise as the wrong train approaches.
That man over there on the opposite platform
Grasps vainly for his placard of title
But the words that made it all up for you
Melt in your mouth, seasons blur
Into a doubtful monotone
And you don't quite know where you are
In this commonplace quarter of town.
Next a kind of enraptured drifting occurs.
The nondescript is indescribable!
You'll rip it up, to make a rag of details.
From nowhere, mid-afternoon, this counsel rises
And the lost novella presses itself to the wall.

27
Wanting to be as here as sunlight
Is, exploding on the brick.
I'll shed this flesh. I'm almost.
Pearls like answers rise unlocked from ocean –
Those people clamped to their seats. O yes
Roses and weddings, an away day.
I want to be here as well, that
Rampage from the beach I carried round.
The dahlias' bloated faces sweat cold dew.
A breakfast of ourselves! Our selves get lost
Like bits of grit among the kitchen things.
A dusty throat so desperately calls
At twilight's verge. We meet in air
I'll want to know which desert we are bound for.

Not Half: The Sixties

Paris France
Passy Passy places
Are tinting on a map. Down by
Contagion immemorial centuries
Corner dust and sun

And a virgin made of gold great counter
And the song of her white tint.
Trees step on forbidden lawns, their
Leaves on the hot sand.

Under the paving stones two faces
Drink choky chocolate and tea.
General society is
The world at the carry of all.

Café Life
The fat man with a rose in his mouth
Hasn't said No yet, she has
Moved from wonder to terror
Seated on his knees.

Her protector
Arriving later with the windows
Breaking a crust at every hour
Goes out to the smoking dog

Past a hospital, that
Monument to fever.
She is an idol
That fits the hand easily.

Lyons Lyon
A girl selling Workers Struggle
Totters under the sun, the city
Roars revolving around her.
Light moves across the facades

And a chicken half-in-mourning for lunch –
It was cold-hot. Coming apart
In the tobacconist's shop
His lenses reflected cigarettes.

Water was coming endlessly from the mouth
Deuil deuil. At Pascal's each noon
Swathes of white curtain hide us eating
Lunch.

Panels

Eiffel Tower O shepherdess
The troop of bridges bleats this morning

Even the cars here have an antique air
                    Guillaume Apollinaire, Zone (1913)

Farmhands bathe the hunting dogs

And not because I could have been
wax angel, evening rain, car catalogue
                    Tristan Tzara, Soir (1913)

And so it happens one March dusk
A bird lifts its voice in the forest-suburb
In the evening's thicket.

Three men are waiting
Like stunned deer round the van
That will not move again.

This is the violet hour
Flavoured with smoke, it has
'The bitterness of engravings.'

As evenings become more spacious
Walkers walk out, like shades of winter.
Each drags along a blob of sunlight

And we will do wonderful things!
Strung out between the bow and target,
Blare of March light in the furrow,

Who quiver with arrows, are rising
From the deep, to mate between covers
In genera. Almond blossom

Brings a warm pink smell to the room.
'We're here to rinse away your thirsts.'
Red branch bends low to catch our speech.

Today will be new
And not in the old way either.
I read that signboard of hours, the sun.

Our sky is not antique
Where its mongrel doves swoop and rise
Before the city's troop of towers –

Those shepherds and those shepherdesses
Prolong themselves on the skyline.
I turned to you, your ways were solar,

Your navel like a winged sycamore key.
On a half-abandoned platform.
Saplings sprang up all around

And I started to think myself
Deep in some forest or other.
Sunlight fell through the slats I walked on.

Almost invisible in sunshine
The signal light transferred itself
From red to green.

Another useless angel passing –
Police car in its stratosphere,
Its siren bubbling like a spring.

Tired of this ancient world,
One body on a million screens,
I insert my card.

An almost human-voice
Tells me a story of money.
A dying pot-plant trails from the shelf

Office-industrial smells,
Photocopier dust, a glare of screens.
A gale of scent steps out of a car

Passing a church that's been
Transformed into a mosque
City being crossed on a hair

On the way up to Paradise
Over the pit and under
Sky's blue capital

The husked geometries oscillate
Settling into a dome, that's been
Restored, to its grey fall of light.

One day I'll reach that undisturbed facade.
It's classical and through the afternoon
Will stay the flow of traffic.

Museum. Stone light,
Where a god half in the river turns
A car going over his shoulder.

Art measures the distance.
Dull clowns at the trough of afternoon
Wear diodes in their hair

Silicon chips for beads
In a city of abandoned trades.
At day's end labour issues from a crack.

Drivers drive past
Whose cars are armed with speakers
And garrisoned with music.

For poetry there's the news
And banditry as art-form.
Graffiti bravely bear away a legend.

The blameless suburbs lie
Elsewhere, beyond a barrier
Of station announcers' distorted greetings.

Where the pleasures of the mouth at dusk
By a gate set secretly in a garden wall
Are our future places in the text.

A patch of lawn, a field of air,
And insects tremulous on each stem
Waiting to inherit.

Last night I stayed up late to write
'The story of my life in the trees'
I drink alone watching the sky for signs

Look into the west, my gin
The late sun drowned in, wafer
That floats up now for my inspection.

Art is a wall with nothing behind it
Shiver in the stream
Trees mediate between the earth and sky,

Such brave signs, crashing in their foliage,
My life being the simplification of a dream
Goes down into its thicket,

Bears with it the unsung portion of my flight,
That sun, mere floating head,
And someone half in the river turns

Behind us certain doors are closing for ever.

Pictures for the City

Early pavement, the
Shining presentiments
Tongue in its hole
Circulating, clucks
Coming again. It foxes

Where the shallow water
Tickled my balls
Waste, the thin track and
Sweat under nylon
Sky pressed its cheek on my
Hand hot and
Cool at the core and I climbed.

Imperfect, the smoke, city
Streets dead at
Centre of cave
Resting on water –
Swell filling with green
Sighs, filling up
With horizons.

Now it's half three, I'm closer.
March upward.
Out on the stone carpet
A dog is improvement.
He beats it still.
At night sky is pressed
On our failing, the centre, such
Gulls and such hospitals.
Come on come in
Little hounds of the spirit, little tongues.
Brilliant Autumn. The wrong
Colour. Dry eye.
Cycle track and an empty pool

For leaf rattle. Treading on our defeats
The huge river engines mounted.

Letter Follows

1
Anger futility spring rains
The sky ruptures water breaks
Puddles on the desk
Mallard descends to the marsh, neck quivering
More water waits by the bole.
Pen nudges the empty paper
Before it's held up like a solo.

2
Now listen, then
Shoot ahead under the wire.
Something alien ruptures the bark –
They cover it up with a crest,
A gloss on the world.
Vaguely in that style you confront it,
The part of you that sleeps or lies.

3
Crossing a depth of ocean
They were much misunderstood.
Now the blue bird of happiness
Says the white girl to the black.
Slowly it rose in a
Sort of shimmer, dissembled meaning
That fell back onto their upturned faces.

4
All the world blows on these fragments,
Forest slopes raising a flame.
They slaughter the lion and go home.
An alien rapture comforts itself
In the rose's centre, in the mouth.
Today the lean almond tree
Is taped to a mirror.

I bought this truth in the rain.
Its strophes so simple and grand
Bore the legend 'I've bunked it six times'.
The playing field's a bleak arena.
I have striven to find some interest
Coming to rest in the forecourt,
Concrete wings spanning the petrol vapours.

Mourning

A flat in North London carpeting the silence
Traffic grumbles in the distance
He deserted me!

Crossing the air
His departure is in the trees
But not human
Scarcely even human

The feet going over the air
And everything burning.
Let me be with the blood

'Atlantic achieved. Scarcely a sound.'

Estuary and Dune

The mingled flesh
First light in the town
Came up to kiss

Where 'plural waving'
Occurred, a slosh
Behind the dunes'

Eyebrow of scrub,
A substance of sound
Alert in the wind.

A gate scraped thirst.
Sea passed between
Confusing the spirit

Slid round in a box
Blossom went dull
Nourishment billowing

Into a mouth
That yawned, inside
Its book of sunlight.

Shadow moved
The fire lapped.
A red car. Bird

Flew across to resemble
The dotted line
On a fragment of cloth

That started and stopped
At the edge of
Nowhere, where

The cold
Diagonals of sky those
Cyclists hurried off to.

My eyes at large
Among the surface –
You're their breathing mark.

I shall go
Up to my room
Finding you there.

A flattened haunch
Of brown is Braque's
'Barque Echouee'

Hollowed out
By paint, a husk
At rest on the wall.

Though the wind blow
Round our tight house
And music fly

This way and that,
Between the folds
Each afternoon

Is quiet as linen
Piled in a cupboard,
Dune's vowel shift

The marram anchors
Belaboured by
The many-sided water.

Neither this way nor that
The narrative act
But divided, divided days.

It's a long time I have been here
Crying and sorting.
At the estuary edge

The clods of grass
Like small lawns break off.
The river dies joined

To the sky by light
Which in turn is
Darkened

By the flocks of small
Waders we'll watch
From our slit of hide.

In Lieu of a Preface

It was some time after the explosion when they all started to arrive, the curators, critics, gallery owners. They sifted through the rubble carefully picking out bits and pieces, brushing the dust off, before mounting and framing them. So it had all happened much earlier than he had thought – this was what he was saying to himself as he moved through the gallery surrounded by cassette twitter, all those other visitors carried along in a trance of information. And here was a glass case where the ephemera were displayed, declarations, manifestos, some printed in heavy *sans serif* type, texts in danger of crumbling, grown fragile as a butterfly's wing. He recalled how, many years before, a group of them had got together to do it all over again. For a time they would meet every week, until the thing came to an end in a series of abrupt dispersals. But it was time to go now. He eased his way through the revolving door and there in the twilight he paused for a moment on the gallery steps and looked up at its classical portico, and then as he turned back there it was again, brusque as an abruptly turning shoulder, moving away through the rush hour crowd.

BLOOD AND DREAMS

THE FISH GOD

'A nibble', you recall, 'but there was nothing there. Then another.' You wondered why it went on nibbling. You pulled in the line. 'My mother was there, encouraging me. There was some reluctance to overcome. I pulled it out and saw how the hook was caught in the gills. But my mother would unstitch it. The river was now a cross between a washing-up bowl and a bath-tub filled with soapy, grey water.

The fish lay there panting, a packet of blood, the blood glimpsed through the gills. I understood that the fish was a tench. It stared at me and I felt guilt at my exploit, but thought I would probably get over this. There was a sense of people in the background urging me on. I saw the fish with a corner of its skin torn and peeling away and for a moment it looked less real.'

You dressed and left for work, a short journey across the marshes. This was to be one of the coldest days of the year, the train as always almost empty. 'At work, before the children came, I had to write out some questions on a story from a reader, and this was the story. "One day Gopal caught a fish. It said, Put me back, and he did so. The fish gave him silk saris for his wife, a house, servants. But Gopal's wife grew greedy. She wanted to be queen. The Fish God was angry and took all the presents back. She went to the riverbank and shouted, but the God never returned. Gopal didn't mind; he just went on fishing."

Over the straight canal
by factories   grass dumb with frost
the train chant and torn seats
smeared felt-tip inscriptions
past the waterworks and the purified river
amazingly clear over gravel, forbidden.

In the market
they were starched in a freezing wind

on the fish-stall: how to fight back
watery tears?

With his baked eye
and the description of his body:
'in the pan silvery side up'

he is the gist of the sea,
the pale thriving bodies.
We shall eat him trimmed, a white packet.
He is pure as a surplice, shorn of his blood,

though as I sliced off the head
the drops of blood welled up from it.

Cat played with this on the concrete outside
her affection sought with the token.

Is it the fish god, his skin
torn, like an envelope?

At five o'clock the Dream Fish
still pulses in its blood
I cross the frost-bound marsh

At twilight   masturbate
the lonely Fish God
in his element
'Marvellous holding their self-born form'.
It takes me back to where I hide
here and there   the room
the freezing garden   the room
a million years. Orphaned and
still pulsing in its blood.
Back to the faint museum
but the Fish God swam overhead.

He is mud-dwelling, widespread
our human stink hunts him
our abbeys of intellect
whitish stone gatherings
wait to receive him,
from cold to cold.
Voices uneasy
out of the flames
are talking of money. Plants
shrivelled by cold
are sprawled on the soil.

He swims
He flies
He lives in the water at night

We eat him.

Fish stood over
the stinking wash. Mother of chaos
sagacious melange of secrets
that spilt. It was named in air
by survival, bursting the skin
of waking
and the guts of the fish just like my own
slither out onto formica
in a heap: cat-coil and cat-shiver.
She gets these too.

But what do *I* do? I go about
all over the town
and write all over it, smeared inscriptions
Aren't pure   Aren't clean

What do you do?

I am baking it in
an oven of blackness, fish is my
teacher and victim. Prudence,
cakes made of sweet terms
compacted in the right way.

But night, the night is
waiting over the roof tops, wine to chill
the slow roasting and melting the transformation
the flames mediate, there is
singing out of the flames.

Fish is altered
'In the first year he came
Fish body but under the fish head
man's head: fish tail
but underneath, man's feet
Speaking like a man
destroying the mind.'

I walked out to the library
through twilit streets, seeking my fortune
in the faint museum of print.

Sky like a helmet, the
final clouds fading
and a last welling up of the light.

Tench
in his midland ponds, in his darkness.

Mud crystal
we all fail.
Imagine

under his roof of ice
inverted world, us passing over
our shadows enormous like clouds.

A TV lay on its side in the grass.

Evening closes the fish eye
and the door in the wall

To drown   in a pool of the sky.

Dragon Dreaming

'To begin with', you said, 'we were sweeping the concrete outside the kitchen with a bundle of twigs, as if preparing for a ritual. When the snake appeared, it issued out from an airbrick beside the kitchen door, next to the vine. I had glimpsed the creature already, coiled like something dead, discarded in the cellar. So I knew it was there.

As it came out we all moved back afraid. It glided over the concrete. At one point it was coming straight for me, head raised and swaying from side to side. I noticed the head's smallness and the bulging eyes black as coal. Then I saw it moving along with the head of another snake emerging from between its jaws. Which was being devoured? Which being born?

Next I was standing by the kitchen door and the snake was moving towards me again. In front of me stood my mother. She was terrified. She reared back, her arms raised in a stance that reminds me strongly, now I look back on the dream, of a Renaissance painting in which a woman is standing over a cradle, part-terrified and part-protective.

But from where I was standing I felt safe, as if there was time to get back in through the door. Then I realised I was wrong. The creature was getting closer, and I wouldn't be able to get away. At that moment, from behind my mother, materialised a tall figure, a woman I thought, but in some way androgynous, who seized the creature behind the head and held it high in the air.

Cloud, and a milky
Curdling in one corner
Where the sun's breaking through

Today on the radio
Earth Wind & Fire
Is the name of a group

Petrol fumes are the mephos
A crushed prehistoric seepage
Fossil to oil: it returns to the sky

His name
Derkesthai: to 'glance dartingly'
Today dumb among ornament

And the river is dark
The reflections in water his scales
Dumbfounded

At the foot of the pillar of sky
Coiled round the base
He lashes himself to a rage

Matings of the eye
Smoke curls away lazily
Over the blackening mirror

Having woken this serpent
Who slept in the measures of coal
He comes out in some glory

And I will walk slowly
Making the most of it
Absenting myself in the song

By mid-morning
Going out and seeing the sunlight
Outstretched on water

That moves so slowly
But does not bear away
What's rooted in mud

The water lily bud's
About to open
The full, dark, pointed head

Just breaks the surface
A mind that's slowly
Lapped in its vigours.

Afloat in scorn, lost waters
Hide and divide in my head

Sulphur-rich city air erodes
The fossil-rubric in derelict gravestones

As I move on emptied of purpose
Hiding my head in his shade

Endlessly feeding him
Notions of order.

Caught in the throat of the dance
I am wearied by such exaltation

At the summit: what am I doing
Tethered to this food grow old quietly

Am such as I am
Enduring though not lasting

He flies through our upper air, beyond limit
Whose script of loyal wings

Leaves instructions on the void
The sunwarmed concrete

I ran my finger down the edge
Of the slab of marble leaning by the wall

Absently noting
The fossils swarming there.

It's the Chinese boy
From Vietnam who tells you
One dull afternoon
In an East London classroom –
You're explaining the water cycle.
He interrupts you to tell you
'I was minding the buffalo
When I saw the dragon come out of the sky
To drink up the sea.'
These creatures, the same boy tells you
Are born of small harmless snakes
Are taken up into the air
On a silent, grey and portentous afternoon
By a sudden lift of wind
You continue to think about this
That descends and then rises
In mediation between earth and sky
As you move to the window, look out
Over the pattern of rooftops.
You look out at space unending
It curves back on itself
And this sign is born of some
Inexplicable fold in the process.
A flock of birds wheels across

The particles move
From nowhere to nowhere
As you return to the blackboard.

A neighbouring dream was one of the stag and the horseman. We were in Colombia; I was walking along the mud of the estuary. A line of fence came down to the shore. Two Indian boys walked along beside it as if announcing what was to come.

I looked across at the hill opposite, a slope of well-tended green. A black stag ran up and diagonally across it, then a horseman, like a toreador, played it. Slowly, stagily as it were, he mounted the creature. This coupling was both devouring and transmutation; now he was Centaur, and he wore the stag's head. He pulled it aside like a flap to reveal his own features somehow formed from the flayed flesh, now emptied of blood, archaic and stern.

He is made
Form, and in filth
Fallen: twice in the same mire.
Now free across seeding grasses, estranged
In a billowing wind. The marsh is whitened
With cow-parsley, elder.
The silence goes out ahead
Bearing his name, sun on his skin
Then radio, thunder, breeze
This trace in dust,
The serpent writing.

Dreaming The Sign

At night: what is told
So, in expectation of night
He is dreaming the sign:

The people in the dream, you recall, were of two sorts: the artistic ones and the ordinary ones. 'The artistic ones all stuck together and held very intimate conversations from which I felt excluded. I was preparing a meal for them all and had to keep rushing off to see to it. But whenever I wanted to start a conversation I could think of nothing to say. At one point in the dream all the artistic ones were collected together in a kind of heap, all in various stages of undress, sticking together like molluscs and talking intensely.

We were in the house of a rich young woman. The space we were in was open-plan and one end of it was her office. It had an antique desk on it with a computer built into the sloping top. There were instructions for making works of art pinned to the walls. She had hardly any books, just a few compendiums entitled Great Novels of the World, in condensed versions. These were packed in the plastic boxes made to look like old books that videos are sometimes kept in. This woman was some sort of entrepreneur in the Art World.

The artistic guests were by this time all looking desperately mournful, though this was, I felt, part of the conspiracy. I found myself looking at a small piece of irregularly shaped black plastic. This apparently stood for one of the Elements, each element having its own symbol. These three-dimensional objects were something more though. They were elements of meaning, each having all the mystery of the sign concentrated into it. I gazed at this one with an intense feeling of longing, as I had earlier been gazing at the half-naked body of a girl.'

Being torn, sky page and flesh
They come on, labial, shining
All the blood of your life
And the sky comes, on a page stiff with gold.

And the snake, you recall, how he shifts in the hut of dream, its roof of scales like letters. 'I am on an antique bike, known as the boneshaker, hurtling through woodland. He lies there, brindled with sunlight. I am going on giddily down to the sea. It is all bright as a new page; these words, word-islands, it was the serpent brought them in, he laid them out in the sunshine, at the edge of the wood, and now he is here once again, coiled across the threshold.

From the fenced woods all around various kinds of creatures came tumbling out. The snakeskin fascia of the dashboard was inset with instruments I did not know how to read.

A tree of broad branches was covered in white birds. It grew in association with the sea. The whiteness of the birds dazzled and the blue sky behind was scattered with fragments of cloud that might have been more birds. There were some binoculars lying beside me. I picked them up to get a better look but the birds all changed to children. Try as I could, I could not see the birds through the binoculars.'

In There
That morning you woke before five, touched by the breath of anterior lives. 'My father had been there. Returned from the dead, he arrived on the fringes of our gathering and was served last, with a glass of neat gin. Then there were various sites; the landscape of me, dreaming, was dotted with these pools. The sun shone straight down into them. Rocks were visible, beneath water whose surface was absolutely still, with a very fine coating of dust or pollen showing in the sunlight. It was not clear which was more real, reflection or reflected. I had to choose one of these pools for a swim, my body anticipating the warm, sunlit embrace, yet there was always the prospect of a more alluring one further on. The dream scored for oblivion: this was the phrase running through my head as I woke up.'

To score being to count by notches
On a yardstick of oblivion
Or else to erase the writing
Or as the meat is scored,
Long lines in the roasting flesh

Or a tune of light, this
Sign of forgetfulness
Incised then dissolved in its radiance –

Sun kindles the water
I wake before sunrise,
My father:
The taste of night on my tongue.

A night wind disturbs the house
I want to be with you
But I cannot explain my location.

Turning on this spot
I have something I want to tell you
                            Flight
Hastens to the tune of my speech.
At daybreak, half bird and half glider
The day has its horn of crimson.
The birds buoy me up
As I enter my fortieth year
Seeking boundaries. It was curious
How a stream of archaic utterance
Like a spine of light bore me
The city below at a gradual angle
My flightpath going over the subtle
Variegations of roof tops
                      Lifted the desk,
Its arching supports tender forms of wood.

The pleasure-bringer has no history
The lips are cut out of an empty sky
Each ones the first, digging one out
Till inward and outward merge, blurred
In the energies of flight
                              Coming down over
The roof tops still as reflections in water
Then a slight wind ruffles dawn's pool
And I avoid drowning
In the pool of anterior lives, I
Coast down now
By billboards bloated with legend
Microdot stars are
Fading points of information.

Against the grain of sleep
I woke to an ingratiating sky,
The rooftops flatter and more unreal.
Clouds beyond them seemed so local,
Sleepy memorial. I have seen
Their white upturned bellies –
It's something I've tried to bring off for years,
This slowly swinging it round into day
Dragging it out from the firmament.
Staring straight into the sun, I remembered
You have to do it because it's impossible.
Now a theatre of cloud moves over his absence
Collapse of all organs into now
As I turn on the hinge of myself
My body a letter bent homewards
Coming to rest on the sill.

Backing off into a smile I greet you
Standing silent in the doorway to language.

Preface, pre-face
Wrinkled blankness
That lay before and turned away

Relating you to dark
The rest of language somewhere there
Blood walks on stilts

To where the mind arches down to
In the lost photograph –
The writing-with-light, the sun-picture.

Saturday morning up early
Postmen quartering the district
As I plunge into street-invaded skies

Fuzzy gold light
And flights of pigeons
Sudden in precincts of stillness

The park's round pool contains
Rubbish and lilies, the tight
Clustered roots and banked growth

Flakes of water, flakes of light
This sense of dissolving into planes
They oscillate gently.

My writing is a turning away
Holding off the pursuit
      By meaning, incisions
        On a surface of water
She was looked on so many times

I fell in the gulf
        Of seeing, passed through
        This crack, my substance
Changed into knowing, smell of a voice
The vein-cluster warm on her.

Plentiful quiet, remote sunrise
Over these ruined fields, shavings of frost
Small incisions on my finger-pads
A blaze of children's voices.
It drifts to a dazzle of silence
Heaped at the window, a signal-burst of sun
Imagined in the course of each slow waking
And beyond that, in snowy fields, a final
Union of meaning with silence.

And so began to describe
Days of pure pleasure, late February
A kestrel, the raptor

In raptures of attention hovering over
The marsh, and oars dipping in water
Blend of activity and calm

How you are seized though not taken
Striving to hold what holds you
Walking backward through summer days, a release

A snipe corkscrews out of reeds just ahead
Standing before the days the children
Are in their bright primary colours

The bird whose wings deride the blue
That seems so sterile here in the new growing
Its plunging body turning into distance.

Sign Writing
This sign and the way it relates us to death, to separation, to otherness

Pre-dawn, I am voluble
Air's charged with incipient grey
A trail of ash on the earth
It is patched with light again
Tattered sentences
Suffused with its energy
In the sky
The incised letters blaze

Now wind turns a page of the garden
Each sign speaks for itself
Opens the mouth of its own stilled vacancy
Studded with all the names
Of its carpet of growth, then walks away
Into silence. The trees
Shoot up again, blocks of
Houses in mist.
You stretch in front of a mirror
Your nightdress beside an opened novel

Large areas have been removed
In a project called Replacing the sky
And did you know which birds
Are omens at large in the sky's page

Wings finger the scales of the air
Finding the thermals, the steep upward draught
All the signs cry out for the key.
Later, for me and for you
        These stanzas, stances.

Local Aspects

It is not only the dream you remember – this dream was, in any case, no more than a single image – but also the moment the following morning when you recalled it. 'I was walking down the road to the station. There were big, run-down Victorian houses on either side. I was just passing a wrecked car parked opposite a breaker's yard. There was dried blood on the windscreen. Next door was a house with a signboard in Hebrew outside it. The house was empty, the paint on the signboard faded and peeling. There was also a synagogue on the corner with a disused look about it. As for the dream: I had been looking at a photograph of a group of Australian Aborigines; a ring of poles with heads and torsos stuck on them and, in the centre of this gruesome circle, a group of women holding children. All were naked save for animals skins slung over their shoulders. They all appeared stricken with grief. This photograph was entitled The Last of the Woodhoppers.

Two things subsequently became connected in my mind with this image. One was a reproduction, which I found among my mother's things after her death, of a painting. My mother was Australian and the painting depicted, on one side, a group of naked Aborigines, in attitudes of gratitude and submission, reaching out in greeting towards a group of Whites dressed in working clothes, while behind arose a dream-city, of sky-scrapers, pure white and wreathed in clouds. The other thing I was reminded of was a group of frescoes by Domenichino in the National Gallery, depicting the achievements of the god Apollo. There the god is shown attacking a succession of primitive, defenceless creatures – the Cyclops, the satyr Marsyas, Daphne and so on. In one fresco, 'Apollo and Neptune Advising Laodemon on the Building of Troy', the god appears as a celestial town planner, as the New City rises, immaculate, in the distance. These scenes are depicted as if on tapestry hangings. At the foot of one of them, and standing just in front of it, obscuring the fringed edge, is a burly dwarf, chained, staring out at the spectator, holding his manacled wrists in front of him.'

Arrivals
But the point of entry
Can't be located, I
Slipped in through the crease, after
Driving through shallow hills
Past a church in a remnant of forest,
Then certain dumb signals –
Garage or public clock –
As we came in against the rush hour
By a wash of houses:
Women escaping from work
Were running across. There was
A migration into the evening.
As in any city of signs, we
Leant forward, face shielded
Against the long-slanting sunlight.
A one-dimensional
Assurance is in the way
People walk here, their turning away
To interiors. Outside
Clouds replace landscape
And the rooftops are like a cutout,
Instantaneous as a transistor.
In a quiet room I am slumped
In a chair by an upstairs window,
All round me
The furnishings of a life apart –
Its sunken glitter. See where he
Steps out into dusk.

A hot wind sticky with secrets sways the curtains.

That evening, out walking past the brick terraces, you sense a special exhalation from these bricks, soot in league with the light. This voice being forced from a rent in earth, this stiffening, separateness . . .
Now you are walking down an avenue of weirdly stunted limes whose stubby trunks are clothed from base to top in leaves that grow straight out from the trunk. A laburnum in blossom. Swifts, pigeons.

What leaches out from these walls, and the new green thrown up against it, like a defence. A drink at the Stag, by the Hospital, the pub's coating of simulated opulence over the ruin. Further on, a man in an ill-fitting turban, no more than a rag wound round his head, stands at the top of some steps and sings, face to the setting sun; a song of such mournfulness, rising and falling. His windows hold flyblown posters referring to some Christian sect. One bears the legend 'There is always room at the inn.'

A huge brick church and round it, mature plane trees. It is getting dark now. A man hurries beneath, has a transistor on broadcasting news, always on the point of the hour. Night-cries of birds in the trees above. In Clapton Square rough-shorn grass and unrestored eighteenth century houses. The trees are still filling with night. People stand drinking outside the pub opposite, at the square's corner; behind them an alleyway of rag-trade factories recedes into the darkness.

Last of all you pass a collection of garages with flat roofs, a slight space between each building, and here a crowd of children are playing a complicated game, dodging and chasing over the rooftops. Most noticeable, as well as their grace, is the constant tapping of their sports shoes. You stay listening there for some time:

> *This then is the first of your lives.*

Misty Roots
Daybreak, and the way in is down the slope of park. The shouts of workmen are companionable in the mist. Someone is singing, the voice rises and falls, and down by the river you'll find them, a clutch of men round a fire of old timbers.

The city: charred emblem.

Standing on the footbridge, on another morning, the sun just up. There is broken ice on the river. The water is burnished by the risen sun, mist drifts across. Such illumination; the post-historic, across it goes our drift. You looked down into the broken ice and water, endlessly into it; everything goes in there, is there and not there.

One day walking along the towpath you looked ahead to where it twisted away into a tunnel, watching the filth afloat on its surface, when you suddenly saw it all rise, it was gulls; as if the whole page took flight.

Night has rinsed the streets with rain; today is mild, a light breeze, the sky astream with light and small clouds moving across; gentle as if washed with eye-water. The willows on the Marshes; a branch dips and sways, the days lead on in a chain, the bushes receding before me. A sense of something gentle but very durable. Soft erotic flare.

The secret architect
Who drowned in his origins

A mouthful of air
Buries the creature
The days are so short, now
Blamelessly the sun expires.

In another season
Returning across the Marsh
In a hot sticky wind

The rain is beginning
Across the reservoir
The moment of it, half-visible curtain
Brushing, then pricking the water-surface
And the smell of it then, rising from pavements.

I mean if you look on it all
With a fair and impartial eye
'I've got a halibut out there' – said, confidentially, to this one
customer. He went to the cold store at the back, and brought forth
the huge episcopal fish. With reverence –

So gulping into wakefulness
Accident victim you swallow your deaths
Estranged in the rupture of meanings.

To Market
The back ways
A wash of streets

Great sun
Valleys of shade

This is the frontage
Of all the cities

Brow braided with railways
Drops gleaming on the bush
In the siding.

Eyes
Screwed up in the dazzle

A fragrant void. Clouds
At rest in a powder-blue sky

Dividedly walks
The shadowed, chill streets,

Street-names are rinsings of the past

Whose saying
Bursts:

A heap of trotters, crusted with a little ice
The broken fish

Kazie's Hallal Meat Co.

Sunlight is edging its way into the not yet open pubs. It illuminates faded plush and suspensions of dust. A Christmas decoration flares in it. This morning is all mornings, it exists before sorrow was.

'Four for a pound them mangoes. All the way from Zanzibar.' Caprice Brand: the dense, purchaseable, odiferous flesh.

'Stop sodding about in there. I remember you, you caused all that trouble last week.'
'Now listen here. It's a new year beginning this week'

Eddoes, sorrel, mouli, Cuban oranges, kolokassi, yam, sweet potato, cabbage, cauliflower, potato, carrot, onion, fennel, pepper, chili, ginger-root, walnut, brazil nut, pecan . . .

        From a wild throat
        Sites of exchange

Commerce sets in motion but also creates a stasis, cutting across the richness and fertility of cultivation, the cornucopia. There is the not-to-be-measured and this measuring that falls across like a shadow. Later there is the sense of a void, an evacuation. At three o'clock a freezing, fraying wind blows us all into bleak statues. Long black Afro wigs on fibreglass stands spiral in the air. Two Reggae stalls at the end of the market seek a way out of this, raising their ladder of music.

The Roads
Zero, and then
The roads
        Curtain
Drawn across
To corner the wind. There is

A pigeon riding it,
Swoops down to settle
Its fluffed-out feathers –
The tarnished famine-brilliance
I needed to be told

Day one. It picks on me.

January dusk, Hackney Marsh
The cormorants are rising off Heron Island
Out in the reservoir, ringed by the city
Black necks stretched out in the
Awkward, urgent flight
They move in a widening arc
Of sexual excitement.

Come back to
Quartered streets
And men of separate uniform
You can't identify –
New brands of helmet, visor
The high hard gaze

Remember you had
Nothing when you came
That way you'll go, gaze
Bolted into sky.

Today I wait on the platform
In the blue vault the helicopter prospers
He can see me down here
Don't worry, it's not you we're after.
The sycamore lunges up through rubble,
Thin drifts of grass, the Carlsberg cans.
Ahead the signal twinkles
In unambiguous on-off language
It's almost drowned in sunshine.
A few scarce points of blossom
Fall through the concrete fence
A train comes in on time.
The one and only passenger
I am now climbs aboard.

March, dusk
Voices wilt by the heater

And out: a guitar
Being plucked in an empty house.
It resonates with the emptiness.

There's a blackbird –
Its startled cry
Heads off into unseen gardens.
Puddles of cold spring rain

So I go on
Making myself
More and more quiet

Splashed with the sound.

Twice-born we move into traffic
Past the flicker of slogans on brickwork.
Cars lumber over pavements
Awkwardly burning the fossil
Fuel, while the gas from those bodies
Is leaking and whimpering through the lead fissures.

Ingestion of poison's a citizen's duty.
Digital time bats a saurian eyelid.
Part of you, taken out, was replaced
By this foliage-murmur
Heat-shimmer on reservoirs
And the flight of a few geese at evening
Across the city, *disjecta membra*
By a dark-leaved municipal shrubbery.

The plane tree flowers are a paleness
In the heart of the leaf-cluster.
A street-lamp on its stilt
Still shines in daylight.

Birds mount through layers of vapour
And a red moth floats
Over the living rail.

Marks that are left behind
When a picture is lifted
Away from a damp wall.

Later the rain starts to fall so quietly
Where a woman leans over a tray of meat.
'This one.' Her downward gesture. Outside
In the road, a dumb fever
On the other side of the window of hours.
We suffer no explanations. Reflections bloom,
Her curving cheek beside the swarming surface –
So be it. Eyelid. Twilight.

Nine o'clock twilight
Blue hydrangea-flare
Beside a sodium streetlamp coming on
This heaviness, faint rain that you can
Hear on the leaves high above
But not feel yet. You're caught
In a tedious web of streets
At a slight angle to the growing night.

On a Sunday afternoon sleep
Waits in my head, and I wake
To walls of pale sunlight
Like an exile float down the street.
Breeze rubs
Its solace of a stone.

Out walking the window's story
Tells each of me who I am.
I reach the reservoir.

Bushes frown beside level water.
Some refugee duck, far out,
Are afloat on the fields of sunlight.

Dull morning of writing-light
Streaked with a sound of aeroplanes.
The flocking birds in their meek insistence.
There's nothing so wild as this decaying suburb.

Breathe in the darkness, breathe in the light,
The thick air of bedrooms, a distance
Of starshine tipped in over evening's orange.

Walking across the city
I came to its dry interior, barred
With an unreadable logo.
There was someone glimpsed in a basement office
Bent over a page of figures.
Girls in their Autumn colours
Strode past above, while the cafe owner
Drowsed by the window. Traffic, a
Chasm of pause the city seesaws over.

A windy day, the page was cleared,
I went out walking,
A van was parked by the boarded-up flats.
The radiant blood of afternoon –
My mind stretched out into its quiet,
Like signs from nowhere birds descended.

'Initial Care is Everywhere.'
A smell of new paint drifted over
As if I were breathing in
The unused part of my life.

By London Wall there are voices
In a blaze of noon once forested
Now stone and so deep in
We're fastened to it
Always on the rim
Of traffic-systems –
Such a heap of fragments
Now the electronic pulse
And an insect-dance of money
This screen-flicker over
The site of exchange, by a river-crossing
A heap of stone brushed clean
And carefully fenced, the withered bargain
That nestles in the fissure.

Seen from a train, the frail
Huddle of houses, that will do nicely –

The bleak playing-fields, the allotments,
Shopping arcades. Down streets

The roses are dusty and flagrant,
All else fails by comparison.

But no one is listening,
Nor could they even hear

Who years ago
Came here by wasteful means

So table the memory-loss.
I do not know the weight of it

As it presses against my side,
But year by year I sigh at what

Such days disclose, in the quiet stalls of air
And so this waste becomes my bride.

By These Waters
Today by the river, between shored-up banks, they are drinking. The flats that rise beyond these Lethean small waters are built like a fortress. The unemployed lean on balconies; words are few, worn-down markers to indicate lives that are shaped by such distances. They drink while the heat increases. The water below them is slothful. Where it splashes it looks like coins. The flats are shelves in the open library of afternoon. Now more and more things seem possible rising on the fumes. On the other side of the river, where pylons cross the marsh, is the site of a Roman necropolis. The power is brought from over there, the merest whisper of it out of the fossil, out of the atom to the machine at which you are working, but still you hardly care.

Circuit
On such summer mornings heat has an almost audible shimmer. The air vibrates with signals. A burnt out circuit lies in long grass, the drops of solder like slow tears. Half-formed musics pour out from the fractures in our lives. A car shifts the sound along; it blares out where the driver pauses. A mural has descended onto the end wall of the

terrace. In front of it is a wilderness of wrecked shrubs and municipal saplings. Sign-boards on small factories blister and fade; impossible to say whether or not they are still functioning. There have been times when you have felt a sort of remote excitement, as if your mind were reaching out to a place where all things touch. 'The lotus is equal to everywhere in the void.' Like a child you learn your way round the streets as if round a computer, understanding none of the underlying principles involved. You return as in a dream to a polished table littered with papers and find your name there, paraph of dust in sunlight.

Leyton Foam
The text's chipped capital: and you go on down the Lea Bridge Road, your resolution weakened by spring gales. Today, smiles behind smiles and you are imagining the bones of Tristan Tzara like some brilliant salty deposit, the glare that comes off them a substitute for light, among the rush of traffic you're dreamed into. Past Brimlake Fur Fabric and Joytime Limited. In hemmed-in front gardens there's this sense of a life all but overborne with its own tremor, and a crowd slow in the streets, its movement grown syrupy with cold in a hollow of the afternoon, a slowed-up entropic carnival that discovers its absence here in the text. The text is almost all margin slowly filling up with bloated signs, messages that will subvert themselves at the twilight's first salute. Slip the halter, you buy the dream, adrift at midday moving between workplaces, a sort of mobile punctuation mark, as if identity were no more than a point moving across a screen at the meeting-place of time and distance, reading these endless legends on offices and shops.

      Occasionally
      A voice of great purity
      Descends

There and Back
You could take a picture, calling it
The First One of the Evening
Walking across
A tableland of park, and now
You're seated by the open door
Inside the pub at an angle to the street.
On the TV screen the multi-
Coloured phantom paratroops
Descend in a blaze of colour,
A frightful parody of Seurat
And all this 'news' leaks out
Escaping among the plane-tree trunks
That are nearly silver, stripped of bark.
A jogger, green on green,
Is dwindling down their avenue.
Crisp packets assault his ankles.
Nearly redundant trains
Rattle into a shallow tunnel
And you remember snow,
How a man, once crossing it
Carried a camera on a tripod
To capture the unsmirched surface
Two winters ago. Pale lights invade
The September evening's final flush,
A time-switch in each streetlamp's throat.
Three men sit upright and alone.
Their faces are hieratic, blameless
Before the screen's hypnotic focus.
So many pictures, entering and leaving
As news slips down the evening's throat.
It does not linger on the
Point of the hour, your gaze
Is always looking back
Helplessly, the moment going.

So you get up and leave,
Walk past the architect's insane
Heaped-up horizontals, facing
Another wall, where Cotton Hand
Laundry is fading into brick.
The van reads Dacca Caterers.
To the east a sky is filled
With towers and domes.

The city is full of meanings but it has no meaning. Everywhere you go there is this sense of a meaning and whole days can pass in your enjoyment of this, but what the meaning is is something that can never be said. Partly it is just the story, the impenetrability of its plotted streets. You lose yourself in that thicket, up here and down there, between desk and pavement. Maybe in the end it can never be anything other than itself.

So, there were those long walks of unravelling, where you went out with no fixed purpose, no special destination, seeking the space that is yourself. Maybe such vacancy was all you sought to lose, then find, your wish being to move through the city simply as a presence, stepping free of intentions and timetables, as if invited to a secret celebration.

On some days it was too beautiful for you to be able to say anything at all, like foliage trapped behind glass. Until this February morning as you stand at an upstairs window, while all around a certain quite definite silence waits. Then it comes, that sense of being here and not here, all things chiming at once in an epiphany of absence, and for a moment you are quite lost in it.

Fresco

1
The dwarf stands by a curtain
That reveals this show.
The sun-god comes
In an abrupt blaze, hunting down indigenes.

The sun-god shoots from the sky,
Diagonal, quick as thought.
A girl flees into laurel.
A stag's muzzle weeps.

These are transformed
Into rocks, boulders
Beside our roads
Existing there
As half-remembered names.
Above the city
A helicopter dawdles.

He shoulders his instrument
To enter the political city, leans over
The media horizon, drying graffiti
While his gaze
Subsumes the glarestrips on passing windscreens.

Bleached flags of last year's carnival
Are strung across a courtyard,
The union jack scorched into brickwork.
He spies disorder in a rift of sunlight –
What's it like to live down there?
He leans against the wall of heat,
Looks up at the cliff of flats, observes
Melanism in pigeons, the precision of footsteps.

2
The word sets out in the sticky night
Down Cambridge Heath Road, Bethnal Green,
Pulse-beat at the edge of thought.
The day's heat does not quit these streets,
It's stored in tilted slabs of concrete.

He floats on these
Where limbs of bronze
Start such desires:

Pausing before the abandoned
Hospital where fireweed cracks the paving
Someone is raving for lack of words.
Each desperate shout in the hot twilight
Is followed by a shocking silence.

Victoria Park,
Entering there, as if on bloated wings.
Beyond the railings
Deer nuzzle crisp bags.
A stag is losing its velvet.
Children with ancient bodies strip and plunge
Into the Union Canal.
It's nearly dark now, drunken laughter
Floats over the shrubbery.

Beyond all this is a wider city
Of shaved brown parks,
Sirens and tourists, then the flickering suburbs.
He takes the last train home
Eyes hunted up and down the carriage
And comes to her at last
Her face abandoned on the pillow,
Aged by sleep:
Shackled, the dwarf
Stands by the curtain that reveals all this.

The Shame of the Oracle

*'Darkness spawning light, night that begets the day,
shame that fractures the oracle's voice'*
　　　　　From 'My Life' by Kamala Das

1
Remembering forebears, to
　　　　Fornicate in a grove
Under an awning of sunlight

Commensal again
　　　　By a shallow lake in the forest
The outspread hand of the sky

Oak leaves float like letters
　　　　On its barely perceptible surge
Leaf-mash below the surface makes

A metallic chestnut glitter.
　　　　He has put on as armour
The brass plate of the sun

2
Their children collect sprouting
　　　　Acorns in motorway-earshot
A voice travels out of a hollow

In such a miasma
　　　　Soaking webs stretched across grasses
Small nets of water

Round them the leaves trickle down
　　　　Graffiti cover the monument
We circle the grove read the signs

Gathering there in the dusk
        Geese feed on protected waters
The fisherman waits

For that mute thing to break the surface
        It will rise into consciousness
It will drown in revelation

The forest border's a wave
        That does not engulf the city
But disgorges riders and walkers at twilight

Into this liminal moment.
        The geese fly over the city
Slipping its halter of lights

Actaeon: transformer
        Who travels but gets no further
In the painted autumn wood

Down rainwet tracks
        A sudden crash of hooves
The water whipped up in shallow frenzy

It's dusk
        The rush hour traffic's piling up
Not knowing what pulls him back

Beside the glimmer of water
        He feels their hot breath closing
Flooded with the unequal gift

He assumes the mask again
        It's about not looking
He turns away to the choir

Of bird song trees in full leaf
        The flight orator grounded
And pulled down into the mire

3
What has been slaughtered in us
        Now rises into its origin
And moves in us again

Between the two worlds moving.
        The chalice of menstrual blood: envy
Possessed this gift

Who calls, who coils,
        Something to move your heart
Less emptiness, more hope

Swallowing, coupling
        Giving birth, devouring
Dressing the vine with ash.

November, and
        Withered by cold
The last chrysanthemums falter

Brought to an inner zone
        Its flayed sky, flakes of sunlight
Struck off the core.

Hurrying to the Underground
        Whether the year opens or closes
Each clutches the badge of event

At dusk perhaps it begins
            Accompanied by some music
So much silence surrounds the music

'Pagoda
            Evenings in Grenada
Gardens in the rain'

November sits in the park
            Beside the abandoned fountain
Where the leaves swirl and rattle

We are led across the sky
            Henceforth by an
Impersonation of the god.

4
Spilt rose of blood
            Bright on the threshold
The virgin seal the icon choir

Such a scheme of silence
            Sings in there
'Fliessendes Wasser: Heil des Mundes'

Gender flow and substance
            Gesture: spillage
Thought coming in the mouth

Labials in earth and slime
            The sky comes down on it
And how this substance shines!

5
Alcohol singeing the brain-cells –
        The night will bring
Its wonders of hoof and horn

The fire in the head
        And the dead piling up:
Parents and dreams.

Sleep on in your house of blood
        Its feathered air, pulse of wings
As in a dream

The Egyptians have come into London
        Flutter of music blown on a stick
Video games by the terminus

And the British Museum like a temple
        Awash with traffic at dusk.
Inside 'Heh God of Millions'

'Four sons of Horus on a lotus flower
        The deceased and an ape adore the sun-disk
Water gods of eternity and the sea'

In here
        Sky-goddess is raised off the earth-god's prick
By a god of the air:

And Hunefer adoring Yesterday and Tomorrow, symbolised by the two lions of the horizon:

That Night

He wrote them all down, the missing
        Fathers so large with their absence
Their dates swimming into his head
        He went to the glass-fronted book case

And took out the piece of flayed cloth
        Its scorchings, incisions, her name
Where it hovered in the air
        He remembered the changing her body gave him

Such a plume of love
        Together nursing unacted desires
Smells of the karma-past. Together
        They forced open the door of light a little.

He looks out onto a fallen street
        Night coming down, in all its shades
Iron or rose in the sky
        That bitter glow not rightly understood

Now he takes down the book of lightnings
        Bound in its shrivelled integument
In the brace of the neck
        A throbbing pain, suppressed angers

'You and I, the skin of a dream –
        Tonight, on this soil of separation
We gaze into the face of love
        Whose child sleeps on unhindered

Night melts in their arrival, who bring
        Wonders, the serpent
Is caught by the throat, held in the shade
        Under the cover of sleep

Not the sun itself, rising, but the moment
        Of sunrise, this fist of light, sperm
Dries on its petals
        He who burns at the door, the name of the herald

This brindled stone of lightnings,
        Tablet of thunder, is born of becoming
How it rests here now in the palm
        Gently, it does not oscillate even.'

He goes upstairs
        Where his body falls back on the bed
November, twilight, alcohol and flame
        They are taking the boat to exile

He opens the glass-fronted book case . . .

Our Mirrors

*I fear the secret of the beloved may become known;
otherwise there is no mystery in dying.* Ghalib

Little sister it has
Ways of becoming known.
Language is its epiphany.

Death is the centre of the grove.
What you are is disclosed
As the small pale tree bends down

And the book is stolen
Quiet as a leaf to the ground.

On Christmas Eve
He wakes up in the failing afternoon
His face turned to the dark side of the year

There is no sign
He says save the word no
Other in the blood

The day dies into orange
All endings fictive:
You must dream it all away

See it flies into the border

It lies
Frozen in such a cradle

Or else cries out!

Deccani Miniature, Hyderabad, early eighteenth century.
Why two, under one
Vine, the fruit split
And the two halves gazing
One girl each side
Of the narrow trunk

They said: caught in the act
Reaching right in and
Taking the fruit

While still he imagines
Her imagining him
In her embrace
As they travel into the bell

What they love for is
A half-remembered colour

'What you grow is young again under me'

Branch
Remember who comes before
The priest makes blood in a cup
In the chalice the watching jewel
Unappeasable her pale border of anger
By the all-smothering vine

Her white blossom dips
To know itself in the garden
Mosaic of beast and leaf and jewel
Now she laps you in that salty quiet
And you are no longer a child

Who calls among the broken vines
Sky stained with the agreement of sunrise
We shall meet again under a flowering branch
How will you be, daughter of that vine
As the scent lifts, drifting away?

Nothing added nothing taken
You are beside yourself
With music sitting there
And watching: kiss the beat
Another world is returning
This time there is no gap
This is all you are for
Regular as the heart

I know you now
Who never in all the years get
Closer to the music

      It is one and one
      It is one and one
      It is one and one

This Other
This other that is
      So like you and is so
Totally covered
      In its skin boundary
That the markers of difference arouse
      Your desire. You turn

Towards the whole figuring
        Of it, from
Fullness to fullness.
        Between here and there is none
Like this that is stretched and folded
        In its play of singleness, swaying
On a lonely stalk.
        A hem of waves withdraws
Under an eyelid of light
        The script of cloud's
A distant incense frozen.
        Around you wind falls quiet
And the squat fruit's carved to stillness
        At dusk to rest
Finally in this other.

Imagination and Dream

1
The city sleeps. One by one
We waken into its dreams
Beginning to dream of ourselves, like children
Throwing stones at a statue.

The word is scrawled on a coffin
Or over a mirror: I saw.
The sleeping town
Is verbal tangles. Although not

Obsequious, not like us, these eat
And breathe and sleep and are without hope
Till going from us
One by one they waken into their dream.

In a sunlit corner of that city
Where I was and was not
I came upon someone fallen quiet
Who was myself and not myself.

Lifting his eyes he addressed me.
'I am beside you now
Riding the breath but not staying.
What you need is this distraction.

When you wake the mirror clouds
With bloom of my exile breath.
You trace your name
And smile into my absence.'

2
I asked if they return in dream.
In dreams they do return
But today
There are so many colours in the wind.

Walking as day breaks in a stone city
To hear the birds all sing away like mad
And so go back there: the lock sticks.
Listen for the faintest footfall.

Raising the shroud of waters
He comes back as I cross the bridge.
So he begins:
'This silver pillar – it accepts my coin.

I've found the charm to let me out and back
Through a gap high in that stained building.'
On the river's far side sun moistened
A distant facade for a moment.

A light wind pleats the tide
Where he crosses into the city –
'I am the horn of change, I fade
Like sunlight from a statue.'

3
There are men in uniforms
That are hard to identify. There is
A smell of singed meat and petrol
Over the funeral carpet of snow.

Light's dragged in through an opening door.
He waits by that suspended entrance.

Corpses of chickens, stained red,
Turn in the breeze that is

Lifting him up beside them.
He says, 'And my imagination
Is not what I'd imagined –
Between the two I fell.'

Whisky and water are the taste of evening.
A live coal rests on lips too tired to explain.
'The hairs along her arm', he said
And the fire-bird fell from its perch.

The truth's revealed, too early to explain
By taking your hand away like that
All that is humanly possible
Here in the old world is waiting for the new.

4
No longer able to transcribe each blaze
You drag the disgraced body homewards
Where daybreak dissolves arrivals into air.
'Once we were awake and now we sing.'

You must dream it all through her mirror.
In her nightdress she arranges herself
In its glass. There is birdsong.
Her book throbs with light in its pages.

Puzzling end-stopped lives.
Some trees inflamed with early sunlight
Hold steady in the painting
Where puce rocks burn by the water.

Out in the street there was something
That lifted away, and the afternoon
Was spent pacing its vacancy –
Pavement, pedestrian pausing, a tune.

Should the dreamer dream he is dead and not wake.
Should he wake and die with that word on his lips.
The fourteen geese like worlds are floating
On islands of imagination.

The Dreamer Restored
'Literature' – like Orpheus as he returns from the Underworld. So long as he looks straight ahead, safe in the knowledge that he is leading someone, it is the Real that lives and breathes and walks behind him, and moves steadily towards the creation of some final meaning. But, should he look round, all he will find in his hands is this meaning clearly stated, which is to say, lifeless.

Daybreak is
Dressing the tree with light

On rising
Their voices, a page, the new garden

Noon   and
The blossom sleeps in the window

Before the face: twinned writings
Mirror the foliage stillness

The dreamer: site of an abandoned cult, come back to daylight. The mark of absence is a blaze on his forehead.

Time and again he is faced with the fact that the one thing he most wanted to say is the one thing he can never say.

The poem, he decided, was about death and imagination and how he existed somewhere between the two.

The paradox is that, denying understanding, he wishes only to be understood, to be visible in the act of flight.

To write – to be seen and yet remain hidden, to be reflected back, a sound of pages being turned in an empty house.

How he suffers in a mirror blind with understanding . . .

The voices telling him, This is your past are all in his own head and yet he cannot believe them because he is still another – he looks back and sees his footsteps filled with dead light.

Saying he does not know whether he writes as an act of self-fulfilment or of self-mutilation; he celebrates the fugue of consciousness, a struggle between naming things and the things being named.

As if truth were a way of not looking, being disguised in front of the mirror; Actaeon, antlers discarded, hiding indoors –

He said:
This dream came before me
There is no unfinished business in the world
Everything I forget I write down.

'I dreamed I had in front of me' he wrote, 'this marvellous text which contained the narrative of a number of my dreams. Each dream had been condensed into a separate phrase and it was these phrases, strung together, that formed the text. Every phrase was pregnant with possibilities and meanings of a magical kind. I was both admiring this text and trying to explain it to someone. The person I was explaining it to may have been Gerard de Nerval, or maybe in the dream I was Nerval. As I woke up, there was one phrase in my head, the only one I can now recall. It was 'The scent of Cybele.' At that moment all I knew about this phrase was that it was not one of the phrases in the text I had dreamed.

Mackerel Sky

A pleasure to watch the mackerel
Losing its silver: colours
Walk off along its back.
It's tinged with blood
Alongside one dulled eye.

Held   it's a slack muscle.
Our earlier loves inside now
Silent on platforms in the frosty air
We watch for yellow letters
On the indicator board,

Open the sunset packet –
A scent of blood and the sea
Moment held in your arms
This bevelled edge
Mirror in the sky you'll tell me.

Ah sweet packet
White then rose were its layers
On a morning sweet with fog
We were in a museum of sounds
On our way to tourist-eroded
Sites – this desire to scatter

Coins over water. They waver
On the other side of surface.
We watch the decay of paint
Colours had fled to the sky
Like alcohol, 'the angels' share'
Into a rainbow of distillation!

Together we move next door
'The Regatta Beating to Windward'

Nearly there, under a mackerel sky,
We wait for our wealth to rise up and greet us.

Still not forsaking the gesture
In the house of words I'd chosen

Writing it out on the back
Of each laurel leaf with my stick

I launched my boat on the puddle
And lifting out the arch of bone

The branch fell brokenly, into exile.
'Reflection is exile' I said.

The crisp rucked-up skin –
Section by section we lifted the side off

Allowing daylight
To ripple across the blind.

THE CONCRETE SHRINE

A Vigil

Typewriter

I can see it crouched there on the table, facing onto the blackness outside. The thing at the back to hold the paper upright sticks up in its V-shape, like antennae. The whole looks as if it is about to set off into the night. Its streamlined blue-grey form is very well adapted. Down below there is a car passing, and then the ting of a shop door. The street lamp is an orange lozenge among the flickering leaves. I am tired and a little nervous. This one has a slim badge of black and silver on the front. There is a sort of handle on the left, looking separate from the rest. The whitish column of the street lamp bisects it. It waits on my table, it's mine, the keys are like separate facets of darkness. Sounds thicken round it – wind, cars, bells, a kind of whispering from the paper. We are departing grudgingly, the typewriter lodged near the leaves, separated only by the glass that imposes a protective barrier.

Cold as earth, curled up among the barking of dogs, the fat machine sleeps among its wheels. Inexhaustible crop, shaken out of the pepperpot. Darkness brushes the edges of the will. Little pagoda on wheels.

Place Bellecour

In that enormous brick-coloured square people are taking the last of the sunlight. Chairs are scattered everywhere, some upright and some fallen – but their chaos does not look unintentional. A small heap of sand blocks my mouth. Further down the road, outside the Cafe of the Four Winds, the rush hour traffic passes. Old women appear on balconies and gaze down at the cars pouring between tall apartment blocks. One by one the chairs are extinguished, some upright and some fallen, their legs sticking absurdly into the air. The reddish sand fades into darkness, my mouth closes; now the night has sealed it with a small heap of words.

August In The Park

The best lines I ever wrote flew out of the window and settled in the trees. In the park children played, their voices strung from branch to branch. On the lake's dulled water the lilies exploded, white and heavy and silent, and when I went out there was mist and a smell of the sea. Then the sun broke through, glinting on the word-web, on the trapped clouds, while from seminar rooms on the other side of the park came voices, sending words across the parquet floor like billiard balls. Some rolled off into a corner where they continued to gather dust for a long time. Carrying on up through the park birds sang to my right and left, mocking my silence. The sun was resting on my shoulder.

Starting To Write It All Down

My face retrieved from the ice of a mirror in a previous house, it was framed in bushy hair, a staring self-portrait. A sense of winter lies beyond the memory back there where it began, growing from a cone of silence, one empty afternoon. A tall, late Victorian terrace, swags of cloud, depending like a pelmet in a room empty of furniture. Now the mirror thaws, cracked ice streaming past, I am nowhere's vassal.

Later I went back, to the house where we used to live, to pick up some letters. I rang the bell and waited for the disturbance behind the rippled glass that would signal someone approaching. I thought I saw it, but it was only the reflection of a car passing in the street behind me. Inner and outer – and I was caught between, as if at the moment of turning a page. Clouds shifted behind me, and then there was a blaze of sunlight in the glass, a signal totally devoid of message. I rang once more, although I knew there was no one there, merely to add my contribution to the growing silence inside before turning back to the street.

Then There Are The Days

The Buddha takes a last secret look at his wife and child before he leaves them for ever. As he rides off, the gods cup his horse's hooves in their hands to muffle the sound.

Waiting for the Sage, up Bamboo Mountain. A rendezvous has been arranged with the Sage but he hasn't turned up. Of course he never will. You look back at the wind in the bamboos, invading the utter silence, and at the blue sky refreshed with little clouds.

There are the days, tell-tale days. In the depths of the tree-trunk the birds, the beasts, still flopping from side to side; sometimes there is a sense of some impossible link being made.

Mopping up the blood, letting it flow back into the roots of the hair, about to be understood.

Emergence

I came out from my hole, from my dust pit, from the rubble and rubbish of myself, like a worm coming out of the ground. I found myself in a field. In the centre of the field was a chair and a man seated on it maintaining a constant silence. The trees were undressing with sly secret smiles.

All roads are the same road. Destinations. We set out in different directions past fallen signposts. I prefer hilltops to valleys, clear views to a dark sleep, and the birds thrown up like a cloud of fertile dust. The sky sends me baffling directives – a twisted tree on the skyline and, when I reach it, the way the sunlight grows into the bark.

Making love, my alter ego waiting behind the screen, she is a mirror of my left side. If I rub her body some breath will cloud the glass. A column, a trunk covered in bark like lizard skin, this is how she was found, escaping from the tyranny of verse.

Behind a stilled screen of eyes bodies are marching down the street, more or less upright. The countryside has had to be tamed with titles

And now the desk is cleared for breath.

Snowfall

As I went outside the air was like a piece of raw meat on my cheek. I saw three generations walking off into the forest. Night, as it fell, added darkness to the trees' dark. Next day the road, going off into a curve of sunlight. Alcohol, the food, the company and the silence after – I imitate a waxen patience. Jointing the chicken, being reasonable now in the tiled kitchen, is that blood on the window? There is still the same even surface, thin detail we have apparently gone down to, and the violence escaping like steam. It's now almost completely dark and the shouting families come back, parents exhorting. Later on, we are sealed in a tea-time quiet, the roads all around us braided with lights. There is something out there in the trees' darkness that testifies, comforts. Next morning, no interruptions, just a dog barking and, at the base our map lifts. A congealed glitter of snow, two days old it was patched with some blueish shadow.

Heart

My head leaning out, like a figurehead, I was flying. I remember the barges going past outside, and how our bodies fought, locked together. Lying in your arms I remembered the sea coming in over a wide beach, erasing tidemarks in the sand, and how the fishes danced. Now as I close my eyes I can see the fruit split open and beside it something beating on a dish. If only we could reach to the heart of the machine!

The Mouse Deer

The trees at this time of year have that worn look, August's roads chequered with sunlight; velleities of the swimming pool under the pines. There were still those moments of panic when you woke suddenly out of an afternoon sleep, the two-sided pronominal identity trace – as if *you* were being recklessly poured into *there*. The signs cried out in a foreign wind. Scatter of leavings that rustles around you at dewfall. Slowly it will get dark and the writing, trailing its wing, gather up the reward of *elsewhere*. Now by the lamp's brightening globe, in the hot night, you are sprawled on the settee.

Next day on the fraying edge of a wood you saw it, the mouse-deer, this alien, blinking in the sun, brought across the border. Back in the city, setting out, crossing the street, the kerb like a comma, the picture's success is –

you, a pulsing murmur, whole paragraphs being sustained in concealment, as you move from pool to pool of the sunlight.

Gallery Hour

In the gallery there are more attendants than visitors on a Monday afternoon. Their uniforms are grey, the carpet earth-coloured and the walls full of silence. An attendant seated in front of a Durer, Follower Of moves restlessly in his chair. He sings a few bars in a quavering voice. The Soul of St Benedict Is Carried Up To God. Another one does the crossword in front of Evening View Near a Village. Two meet by a doorway between rooms, and at this boundary discuss the previous night's television. The water is in motion, pouring across three canvases. Playing at Bowls and The Conversation are by Teniers, the latter a wind-bitten scene, pale sunlight and an old man disappearing off to the right. "I see you've got a relief next Sunday". It is four o'clock now and they all begin, almost imperceptibly, to stir, as if the day were changing gear. We stare at a piece of grey and brown canvas –

>'Small Vessel in Light Airs'

Two Statues

Her face is small and brown, the nose straight and rather sharp. The eyes are painted in. Her thighs are long and slender, her hands and feet delicate. She is remote from us and the man beside her, broad-shouldered and narrow-waisted, is holding a curved axe.

Her sister, who is younger, is very white and pure. The folds of her drapery are complex, her thighs full, her crutch modestly shielded. Her arms are full of metaphors and in her head-dress bees make their honey. She is a scale of measurements and her body is a set of rules, severe and exact, displacing the air as a ship displaces water, filling the void with a type of abstract amplitude.

Later she returns, in a new incarnation. She lolls back on a sofa, thighs apart, head back, where the salon spectators gather. She is Art. She is relegated to academies and to public squares, to cupboards where the spider weaves in the fold of her drapery, and we hear her archaic sister call to us, over the bitter sea.

The Assessors

After the various deities had departed from their images words settled there like flies, blackening the stone. It was a time for reassessment. Dust filled the air. It settled and we sifted it through, looking for clues, looking for a place to sleep. The city was spread all around us suspended from wires. It was no more than an idea now resting on its rock like a butterfly. I saw a man coming towards me holding a shield. Together we began to build.

After the statues had fallen, assessors came, righted them, brushed off the dust and turned away to their calculations. They were concerned solely with measurement, the distance from nose to lip, from eye to finger. There were timetables to be drawn up, museums opening and closing like bivalves, and the day to be divided into segments; like this there would be something for everyone.

I looked round. There were two birds resting on her shoulder. I lifted them carefully off. They turned to clay and fell apart in my hands. We worked. The stone sang in the clear morning air. The birds come back each night now. I lift them off and place them in a corner near where we sleep. Each morning they have gone, only a handful of dust remains.

In the pinewoods steel and titanium were exploded together. The bond is inter-molecular, beneath its shroud of sound. Libraries are being installed in the cracks. Books multiply in the shelves like millipedes.

This morning, the house was finished. We moved the furniture in and settled down to a meal. Through the window we saw the statues flying, always further off yet apparently motionless, over the trees and each in his own time.

Passing The Time

Scrutinised at daybreak the text clears wonderfully. I can understand anything! I wrote it down not daring to look back. By the ever-faithful tide a bivalve hums with radiant energy. A bird calls, its brain seized with light. The shorn notes are scattered on the ground, shavings from the once and original rule.

I am straining, I am attending. I am in attendance. I have heard of nothing and Nothing has heard of me, my body at an uncomfortable angle to dust and speed, water, wind. A day seems mine for the taking. Wet the edges and press down firmly. Buds shed their covering as I come closer, tapping the keys, bowed beneath the weight of this diurnal oppression.

A surface-noise of leaves. Journeys to the periphery – but never, so far, the unsoiled adventure. But once as I sat in my room at midnight such a sensation of power; a hot summer night and the surge of traffic below me, I was the city and I could do anything with it and I wrote it down as if it wrote me.

Junk shop inventory: a few old novels in the doorway on rickety shelving are fading in the unusually strong October sunlight. The exceptional nature of the weather contributes to this sense of timelessness, of images beating back, however hard you try to move forward, so that before you know it the moment has passed again like an arrow into what you are.

A stream of office-workers hurry along the path through the graveyard, past thin shaded vegetation growing on the far side of the railings. The builder's arm had a tattoo Death Waits For No Man. Beyond him new tower-blocks rise blank as pearls. Even these concrete boulevards you study must have a life going on near them, a microclimate with its sunlight and its fogs and, one inch above such surfaces, the peace that passeth all understanding.

Outside wind lashes the remaining leaves, a depleting theatre of gesture. An actor looking down from the walls is saying As the years go by even the pines in the picture grow old like the real ones. A flake of snow is all the difference.

A sense of there being so much, and of the gulf this creates. You can never quite reach across to all that abundance. The loaded branch comes down to the water. You are between branch and reflection, striking in at a tangent. Dumbfounded by this excess, language seeks to redeem itself by its superfluity.

Bride of the void, guests at a meal, feeding in absentia.

A rain of colours, and then the pale litany of the text.

Shores

Waking early, the hurrying clouds, watching a white mist curl down the hill, sleeping and waking again and you look, the way it fades, how the whiteness disappears. Finding out what you are, to fill the dull spaces. There is this aperture admitting light, that sleeps and then, after waking up to observe the muffled brightness, will sleep again

Curled around itself. A blackbird meanwhile is in the bushes, under sliding screens of air. The bush borrows some wind, the bird sounds. Sheet upon sheet of things seen, reported, remembered.

Or do you propose to be where you are not? Buried deep in a sofa, dozing behind the window, or in the garden grown sullen in a sea wind? While we're still here, storing our bodies here, one day we shall be here naked as lightning.

This afternoon we have come to where the sea begins, beyond a long tongue of shingle. Here, it is legion and we are marginal. Coming over the water now a little sunlight was released from between the clouds, and the slopping bumping grinding goes on towards a very definite line of horizon, waves crashing, some more sunlight in a narrow path just touching the tops of the waves, a little more squeezed out as from the mouth of a purse. After last night's storm the beach is littered with the white bones of cuttlefish.

As if water, at rest in a bowl, were brought here and placed in front of you. Sea-campion, the stone where it shelters; it has colonised the stones and now it binds them together. Familiar with the salt winds the withered plants are our dried-up secrets as we set off home, a sea mist moving up the valley. On the kitchen table you lay the four flatfish, gutted, and tidy like mittens.

The Singers

We can hear them singing, each one in a separate room. Their song is something between pure joy and a scream, and they never stop repeating their song. As I walk past it seems torn from the rooms that rise above us and fragments of their song float out of a half-opened window. They sing, their wings stitched to the walls. This is their occupation – no point in questioning their motives. Perhaps it is a kind of penance. The building is a honeycomb of rooms and each has its singer. But, if you go in, all you will find is one or two strands of hair, part of a violin, or perhaps the torn fragment of a wing.

The Vigil

I went out to post the letter. Passing overhead the plane briefly lit up a cloud. Twilight, the hour of traces – and finding even this bird has flown. In the story the windows all opened inwards.

Always wanting to know what is *written* there – on badges, plastic bags, T-shirts. Trying to manoeuvre myself close enough to see without being noticed. My greed, surrounded by all this textual restlessness – it is the surface of print I am drawn to, not the immersion into narrative.

The wave-worn seashell, robbed of its one foot. The planes make noises off. One of them briefly lit up a cloud. Now, the hour of traces, we are let loose in the pattern. My daughter shows me a pebble, husk of the wave, a dry sparkle still to its surface.

As the doorbell goes she calls and I call. In the end I go. The boy is leaning against the side of the porch, faintly menacing for a moment, bringing the city in. All this going in and out, curious blank days. Leaning on my desk – beside me there is a novel 'The Naked Passenger' – while outside light fades on arterial roads.

I go out to post a letter, in another version. By the Victorian pillar box at the end of the street, a middle-aged man comes up to me. The pillar box stands askew, a battered piece of street furniture. The top looks like a plumed hat, solidified. The man hands me paper and pencil. He tells me an address – not somewhere round here – and asks me to write it down for him. All this part of the street is flanked with corrugated iron. Beyond it the clouds pile up, and weeds bleed through from underneath. Twilight begins to seep into the picture. I turn back from posting the letter. Briefly the plane lit up a cloud.

The owl, stripped of its flesh, is a faint shine on the paper. The two huge eyes still gleam as if rubbed bright. A boy runs into his skeleton fleet as the wind. My guts are coiled inside me like a sleeping child. With his scalpel the artist had moved aside mountains of flesh and rendered it down to this liveliness walking the page. He is a shoulder in the crowd. He has come to talk to me. I confront him with my carefully cultivated vacancy and now he is marching away from me, carrying off my hopeful smile.

The barber's shop at 4.40 PM. The shop doesn't have a pole, but instead diagonal red and white stripes have been painted on each side of the door. It is empty and dusty sunlight shines into the room. A radio is playing. Around the chair piles of hair cast small soft shadows.

Over the street now the cumulus glows bright at the edges. Ridges of shadow deepen along the corrugated iron around the building site. A car is approaching the garage on the corner very slowly. The young man in the barber's shop next door, slumped back in the chair, exposes his jugular like an animal. The card-players near him are frozen for a moment in their never-ending game. Next there occurs a slow motion falling outwards as if from a still centre and it all starts up again like a fountain, water rising and sinking back.

Dot! The vertical cleanser. I tried to describe it, harassed continually by the stripes. The person who helped me strove to achieve his own significance. I wanted his voiceprint, his fingerprint, my fantasy about his reality. There are brief descriptions that hug the fleet skeleton. But I can't put in everything – I have to give as few clues as I can get away with. Someone waits beside the unchanging conifer, in rain or sunlight, the ground shrivelled before his spectral attention.

The lamp lit from inside, bottled thought. The sunlight it contained had all been consumed, vomited up, and the lamp, still sleeping, was believed to be part of the struggle.

Outside, meanwhile, I was not invited to the party in the park, nobody was though everyone was there. Groups lingered on the fringes of other groups, rotating slowly like cogwheels in the summer night. On the way back drinkers were congregating outside pubs and children crouched in doorways played cards, though it must have been long past their bedtime. Girls giggled in the dark, a child called out in its sleep, still the voices debate and will do so for ever, or at least for as long as they can, calling the lamp as witness to their sleepy listenings.

Though in the communion of objects it was nothing special. Not even a smoking wing or trail of blood across the carpet. People had wished to pretend that it was – its very brightness was held to be a kind of witness, filling the curtains with light, curtains that billowed round enormous invisible struggles while outside the sky grew pale with thought and the trees swayed in the dawn wind, seeming to listen.

The Storms

Something bad in the sky
Like a yellowish bruise.
The stain is spreading.

The florist waits in her boutique crowned with flowers.
The charcutier reposes among his pates and hams.

The storm gathered over the housetops.
You stood by the window head bowed.
When the storm arrived
We were there at the station to greet it
With our drums and flags
And the mayor made a speech.

Love stepped out of the train
Hand in hand with love, devoutly twinned,
Two names written in one face,
One in two and two in one.

When the storm approached
The leaves began to shiver on the mountain, turning their backs.
In front of the cave there were ice-cream cartons,
Cigarette packets, the traces of a fire

And below us
The lake shaped like a boomerang
Changing from blue to grey to brown to green.

We had finished all the wine.
We gathered under a tree to wait.
When the storm arrived leaves rattled.

At the base of the mountain
It struck, took root like a footprint.

Each day it's the same now,
Stifling heat, greyness, sky like metal that someone has breathed on
And sometimes in the evening a dribble of rain.

At the centre of the stormcloud there are crystals of ice.

In a city ringed with mountains
The storm shone over the edge of the mountain with a muted light.
'These are stormclouds' he said, 'I know it'
But the storm changed its mind and moved off.
The river raised its head,
The river, colour of slate, rushed through the city
Past the electronics factories, past the centre for nuclear research
Hurrying reflections out of the city,
Carrying poisons, river
Tilted at an angle.

Children scooped up handfuls of dust from the road.
Houses were rising fast as light.
Students chanted slogans.

Balanced on the
Edge of the freeway that
Runs off towards the
Mountains.

We ride on the
Edge. It tilts
Carrying us past new
Apartment blocks.

Around them, waste ground
And tall grass.
In new rooms the storm sings.
It sings in the taps

To the right there is
A barricade, there are banners.
At the top of a towerblock
Students wait for the police.

They have taken trolleys
From the supermarket opposite,
Loaded them up
With stones.

The storm sings
In a world
Brittle with newness.
We ride on the edge.

In the hospital a child has been born
And her five year-old cousin asks her mother
'When I was inside, did I walk around?'
And 'How was I fed?'

The storm came
With so many questions
I had no answers prepared

And the dust was full of questions
Where the wind raised it
Blowing sudden and cold.

In the doorway we said goodbye to the grandmother
Where she lived on the edge of the city.
She turned and went into the empty house.
The tall grass swayed
And the night came on, over the fields.

City on the edge of a lake,
Houses going down to the water.
An osprey float out from the shore.

Found only in the Lac
Du Bourget, fifty metres
Or more below the surface

The Laveret, fished on a line.
When brought up to the air
A change in pressure bursts the brain

It comes to our table
Sliced and draped
In a wine and cheese sauce.

The flesh is dense and tender
But I have eaten and drunk
Too much, the air

Is so heavy it's almost liquid.
My body's awash with sweat.
O to be pure again

Like the fish in deep water
At ease in his own world.
Beside the restaurant grow

Vines, and some fig trees
In a cleft in the mountain,
Their success a trick of the terrain.

On other side of the lake
The rocks go right down to the shore
And there isn't a road.

Standing in boats, fishermen
Are attentive, their rods
Poised over the water.

Lying on the bed
My body was like an unwinding string
And ragged curtains of rain
Were blown past my window.

Before I slept
Rain was striking the street,
The thunder walking around in the sky.

If I could convey
The scent of the rain
Coming in over the town

But the most we could do was
To hold it for a moment
Before it left us.

The most we could do
Was to count the pieces
Stringing them together,

To have
Something to remember:

The river scattered in pieces among the mountains,
The storm resting among the vines.

    Lyon / Grenoble / Aix-les-Bains / Lyon

On Skye

One walks with oneself in the rain.

You are trying hard too. You are doing your best I think. It must be difficult. I am getting on with my inventions. I am trying to prop things up. The sun comes up to inspect my pale girders. Along the branch are berries of rain, and the flower collector is out there too – he has defined an area of innocence all his own. The flying collector? The berries of rain can harden, you'll see.

A little hill of sea, castle without a door, then the sawn-off land approaches. Patches of grain appear and hay, piled in the fields like hats. A thread of water runs secretly through the grass. Then sun: its orange stance.

The small white houses were a long way below, an amiable solidity, smoke drifting up from one corner, and when we came down off the hill, it was as if everything familiar had been washed away.

While off to their next destination went the motorists, feeling the flow of miles and hours, floating past the millennia of rock. Winds, clouds in the cradle of change.

Sky went dark then sunlight appeared again on the lower slopes which were speckled with flowers. From out of a cleft, its steep sides green with bushes, I held you. Quartz blink: we contract, into a ball of air.

Unable to get beyond this, and the miles and miles of writing. So what is out there? We eat then look out at the rain-shod clouds marching up the bay. So what takes place? Only rain and this endless water farming the beaches.

This, and the
Orange seaweed like hair
Lying back, on the
Whitened serious stones

The people who live here have little interest as a rule in walking on the hills and regard their huge bulk as no more than a tiresome inevitablilty. One day though we did meet a boy up there, the son of a crofter, who had decided to make the climb for once. Side by side we stood watching the curtain of rain blow across the rockface, and beyond, on the sea miles below, patches of sunlight waltzed across the sea's dulled silver. Homewas imagined all the way down the hill. It was difficult to say where the sea really began, land and water being so interwoven, in a complex system

Of lakes? Like this they began their humble conversation, water, land, land and water. Where are you floating now? I push through the long grass to the village of your miles, the hill's plaid adrift in momentary sunlight. A raven, up on the cliff, alights on its shadow.

The evening settles down here like a large, quiet bird, then seems to pause for hours. A bush by the roadside – its long grey-green leaves are quite still against the loch and, further down the slope, a single meadow gleaming.

Coffined in sleep, you fly with the winged island.

The disposition of boulders, on the face of the hill, stones in sunlight. A trace of cloud on the mountain. Next, to it is a dark pool. I have been moving around this place for so long. We are solitary vectors, visitors on the hill. Our aloneness vibrates on the stone before being still. Any prison is good enough to watch the world from.

What the eye harvests and the patient ear collects. Water that gathers in small reflecting pools. Facing extinction, it will fade away quietly

Is an oxeye daisy
Or is an eye still humming in the sea.
Between us the stone, warm, resting under water like a sleepy shark, a longish rounded green syllable.

There is something that happens because it is here
Where sunlight rests on its stone of extinction.

He had got his life to such a pitch of precision that there was nothing left save the sound of wind in tuned wires, out there on the mountain or blowing through the thin ancient grass. A long slope, then bounding over the small cities of moss that simultaneously thrive and decay. To the left, through mist, a river slithered over its tables of stone

> The rags of rain
> Before behind around –
> The further land was sunlit
> A face through tears.

Coda: on Harris

An enormous sweep of estuary, and the spiky terns, furious in the wake of retreating water. Ahead of us there stood a flattish island and to the right, blue empty hills, afloat in the lens of distance. These were the Hebrides; this the Atlantic – recognition, strut of the world where we are alive and well. Reaching the headland, we bathed naked in the long waves, being merged into the seamless dress of air, the long drawn out and endlessly breaking water, our bodies, coffined in ocean, dragging like curtains.

The Concrete Shrine

"You want that paper? The Telegraph? No, please buy it. If you don't buy it I will buy it for you. I tell you, this is the best periptero in Athens. Tell me, where do you come from? Ah yes, which part of London is that? Do you mind if I walk with you? You do not. Would you like to smoke? Do you mind if I smoke? You want to eat? I tell you where to eat. Here is the card. Go in there and tell them my name. My name is Sami. Here, I will spell it for you. S is for Sign, A is for Alpha, M is for Man and I is for Item. Go in there and ask for Mr Vassilis. Do you mind if I walk with you? I am Greek and I must tell you I am ashamed to be Greek. No, you are right, you must not trust me. Do not take your hand away from your pockets. I tell you, I am the worst man in Athens. You are here on a tour? Key Tours, CHAT Tours, Cosmos. You see, I know them all. Here, you want to buy? No, please, I insist, just to look, not to buy. These people are my friends. Here, give them a discount – 50%, 100%. All right, we go down there. Do you know bouzouki? Do you mind if I walk with you?"

Remember as we came
Signs bobbing over concrete –
GOODYEAR HELLAS HOOVER,

Wonky roadside shrines
NISSAN on a concrete block
In the middle of a field

Precisely nowhere / seven miles to Thebes.

The rods stick up through concrete
In half-built villas here and there
Waving their rusty stems

And, as we pass,
Imagine I am this other, seated
Under a living awning
It might be of wisteria

In some such dusty half-built town
As we keep passing through,
Emigrant not colonist,
Not like those others, setting out
Once, cities under the prow.
Here, oranges glow
Hung lamp-like in the upper branches.
Scent wafts from blossom lower down
To blend with diesel.
"There I'll sit and sip
Watch as the night comes on . . ."

           Today
And still in the bus I'm feeling ill.
I get out and stretch my legs,
Eat bread and meat, under a leafless tree
Pale in its armour of sunlight,
Look up at mountains –
        Olympos

Then a hill-town, rugs
Spread everywhere across the road

A concrete church, its flattened dome
And on the hillside, concrete hives.

I paused, the whole tree humming,
Pine heavy with its fruit of sound
In front of the Museum at Delphi
That still grey morning

'Le bourdon, tu entends?'
She pausing likewise
On the ball of her foot.

Back in Athens, the *mephos*,
The fossil brought up from clefts in earth
Emits this brown glare on the skyline.

Down there the taxi driver.
He had two radios.
Through one he spoke, to one he listened
Moving slowly into
The tide of metal.
Up here it's twilight.
The sale of tickets ceases.
The music from her radio
Is cracked and rasping –
It joins us to the city down below.

White city, hill
A broken skull.
The polished marble pieces

Paved our ascent.
Here at the summit
Flaps the national flag.

Cards proclaim the strike.
One has blown here
Rising and rising on a hot wind

All the way up to where
The Germans sit and drink their beer
Brewed here under licence.

Down below, the city
Extends towards its rim of hills,
Limestone blurred with a grey scrub,

Small concrete blocks and half-made roads,
Traffic dust and music,
Carpets hung from balconies

As if spattered with blood of the sun
And here and there rough glitter
Among the concrete-white.

Turning the other way
We can just see the island –
A shadow, that we visited.

The lottery seller came as well
Carrying his staff of numbers
Into its salt of light.

The boat departed.
The evening chilled
Where in the gulf a sunset hung, becalmed.

And now small girl's carrying out a candle
Of sallow wax the colour of her skin
From inside the shrine.

Beside me hangs a telephone –
'Information –
Where to go and what to see'.

It's in four languages. I'm tempted
To lift the battered oracle,
Hear what it's creaking tones rehearse.

Instead I go inside
And drop the last of my small change
Before the picture of a starving child.

Sounding not quite real
The light coins rattle in the tin.
Where we descend

Someone has written
Engraved in the living cactus
Lebanon in my heart
      Athens / Delphi / Athens

What He Said

My father, how poor my dreams
Show me you have become

The sperm track
dawn sheet

shell of the sky growing pale
it rubs out the dead

Alone on a bed of light
all by himself he calls his tune

pauses its
 I start here.

His face is distant. Heat-shimmer.
Walls blacken with my text.

The season's a lush grid.

Solely the wind
is the ragged power
in the pleats of their skirts

splitting open the bags
and pulling out more material
reams of stuff like flags or bunting.

She presses her tummy
a famous disappearance
fingers the tweed

Days of rain and heaviness
   we read each other in darkness
have children
   and I am the hinge

As I turn towards you, the sun
comes up behind my shoulder.
The baby stirs and snorts in his basket
   five a.m.
the sun at the window, risen
   over our scarce wet grass,
and ancient weeds that flourish in brick
   to make a thin salad.
Now the whole sky it fills
   with a roar of timetables

Matisse: 'The inhabited
Silence of houses'

and then the opening door, clouds
pour across.

A threshold holds off grass.

Our handkerchief of garden
changes from moment to moment

and you and me, vulnerable
in our identity of want
are turning back, each to the
painted darkness inside

I bath I drink and eat.
the ritual the flow the stepping out into

Funny grey windy weather
pale heat with its hint of sun.

Cow parsley, reservoir shimmer, a flock of sparrows
veering away wheedling.
Almost derelict stations –

Queens Road Walthamstow, Clapton.
The concrete splits, showing green veins

    And at night
the air is still scented with
some almost forgotten industrial process.
Pale new leaves of lime
spill out across brick.
Huge irises shine behind railings

The going out and in
the cool to bright.
A shadow swells then shrinks.
Breeze rattles the window.
Today
graduate of dream looks out
over the ruined gardens –
ragwort, sunlight.
The rough grass streams

Perfect early summer
and pigeons go high in the trees

Perfect early summer
the familiar is noble green

Days of this thin high cloud.
We are moving yet perfectly still
where along a flickering edge
the wind grows calm

The bleached forecourt of noon –
Coming back home
Sounds are a picture
Framed by an open window

Five cats on the dusty earth
in the hottest part of the day.
A girl eases off her tights
on a patch of grass.

A car at the end of our street
though moving seems motionless.
Evening and morning I wait for you.
Our paths cross a hundred times in a day

What I want to tell you and not
testing the words against paper

Screwed up like handkerchiefs inside the bud
now the poppies are
a constant stripping inwards.

At the periphery of vision
I can see their petals
flutter down, catch in the leaves.

A long way off is a siren
dividing attention, we are other.
and we watch ourselves merge into detail.

The poppies, as if my gaze
slow and absolutely direct
petals still trickling down
might have outstared oblivion.

It's all an arrangement
of clouds and houses:
the what-happens-next of your life

you teach yourself how to
manipulate this ripple
flag that empties itself into air

And after three restless nights
I woke up still unsteady.
The new tree cast its shade on asphalt.

The pavements rocked under my feet
walking past booths of music
bushes festooned with drops
and everything at work, a lake in motion

I come home down dusty streets
indoors all weekend.
Going out again

this amazing tinsel shimmer
bringing me back, then days of rain
and yawn in the cavity

Arranging appearances
a life is the sum.

But with art the whole thing
Thickens. I graze the paint.
The living author
encased in text-armour
marshals his anxious brilliance

The swifts a long way up
are swimming in a warm stream
of air and insects

sometimes descend
to garden and house level

while down here we hold
a vigil of all the pieces, afraid

Harmonie du soir, the clouds
pile up
and each dulled flower vibrates.

An evening of alcohol
will blot out recollection.

Anyway water the yellow and purple.
It won't rain yet.

A gentle heart the empty bowl
I assemble each vestige of yesterday's brilliance.

Weather forecast says, sunshine
out on the coast. I imagine
dipping into it on the plane's journey.

Down here records shudder
sounds and perfumes. Nothing carries us off

But the weather changes, bringing
a shift in focus and energies.

Take in the yoghourt and
into the airing cupboard.

The stiff trees the settling voices.

Ice cream chimes and church bells.

You have just arrived
I stretched out my arms to greet you.

The Following
On a Friday evening in summer
Tired faces hang in the dusty glass.
They hear the word spoken in empty places.

An advertisement rears up over the grass
And the grass prickles up through the bands
Of shadow being laid across sunlight.

I am trying to find something
That will strike in just so, at an angle.
My tube train glides past iris and lilac.

I walk up the street in a daze of watching
This hybrid swarm in the thickening forest,
Inspecting the dappled surface, following

On Orkney

(Our) Island Selves
'No man is an island', but an island certainly is. A comparison with the Cyclades, thinking of the wealth of ancient remains in each case, may seem fanciful but there it is. The Cycladic island of Delos, birthplace of Apollo, was apparently an island that moved about. 'Delos' means 'obvious' and after all what could be more obvious than an island? 'Island' equals 'significant'? Meanwhile we are all moored in shifting ocean, and daily inspecting our borders. As for the Orkney ruins, they are for the most part eminently visitable, often to be found on a not much visited hillside, and one can spend a good deal of time squeezing through a variety of orifices to investigate the interior stonework. The Orkney island of Rousay was described as the 'Egypt of the North' in one brochure I saw. We spent a day there walking its length and coming back I remember getting inside the tomb half way along (there was naturally a boat to catch) and I looked out through its slit to see what there was of the world. As if I lived in that crack, getting inside the story. Meanwhile there's the thing I find on the beach, wood, shell or stone and because it pleases me I take it home and wonder, did I choose it or did it choose me? By degrees the thing moves into focus. 'Our island story' you might call it.

'Still Life', blind sculpted head.
There it was in a painting
Perched by a window   a gulf of seeing –
It's Aberdeen, the gallery.
We're waiting till the boat can take us.

We'll arrive where the sculptor has come to roost
Here at a different edge
Where the dog's bowl stands on the flags in the hall,
The dog's bright bowl, it shines with nothing
And outside the miles and miles of air.

'The dog's eaten half a curlew',
Gobbled up its cry.
He'll chase a gull out into a waste of water.

Once here there is being without effort
Each day taking the mind for its walk:
Look up, keep
Watching for that incidence of blue.
All we can do is gaze and here,
Here is 'I' at the worn stone of going in.
Stone of beginning   skyish stone
And being out of so much stillness made.
I'll look at hills

Or else we'll drift along through morning mist
Mournful calling of seals out there –
I found one of their skulls.
It is as if I've moved
Among discarded things
Growing into the world
Taking so many meanings into myself,
Bird vainly flying
An attraction to surface
Roughness of that antique coin
I brought here with me
      Cirrus
  Am consecrated
Awkwardly, here in the gathering
The language a calling to itself,
It brims its depths.

There are munching armies
Out on the wind-filled
Slope of hill,
The open sky, its compilations of clouds.

Walking on islands,
Blue day and in it
Up to the hilt
The faint shore's almost
Everywhere I look.
Schooling the breath
Time's the faint dragon
I saw almost gone on the stone,
Where is there room for all the bones?

Eye moves to a surface
Where jellyfish is a splash
Of translucent pale purple,
Odd diagram of life
Stretched on the rock of afternoon.

We who will be replaced with
Something so much quieter than us.
It will be finally
Too much to hold
Here on the quiet islands –
My feet clatter, incoming
Tide's just a shimmer among the boulders.
The birds fly off with their names.
An evening wastes its calm.

The first time here   looked still and hard
As if willing a sky
Burnt August grasses
And the sea being ultramarine,

Sightless extremities
As if it were all
A matter of digestion

And the watcher come to the hill were saying
'Leave me to my appetites!'

And I had schooled myself
To an absence of expectations,
But Cambrian salute – the world
Entire it is all
Familiar with itself
As if I am the piece of grit in its eye.

I being at miles with the stone
Am walking around a small lake.
The bird out here on the hill
Who watches me from his scoop of water,
Snake-necked he dives and I am
Left with a blank page of water,
Dark ruffled sheet of silence.
He had a moth-eaten look,
Being of a grey-brown colour.

Next day approached the village.
   In blew the name of sand.
How can the day be here again?

A stone rallies distance
   And the way this lintel
Sits here like a pillow

After five thousand years –
   It has a certain
Time-cancelling quality,

Impacted, the
  Stone pages
Their runnels of erosion,

Being lifted each
  Up against sky to
Make sun-linkage

Just next to the waves
  As when the first bird
Swam into stone, it

Seems like yesterday
  And weighed in the hand
Is the peace of an axe.

Noon-sprawl   the moment
  At ease with the dead –
A cliff topped with flowers

And all that sun-dark rock below.
  There is so much driftwood
Come to the beach down there,

Hinged evasiveness
  Of the pronoun,
Sea eagles, brought into the cave

Abrupt as flight a gull
  Invades your driftwood pieces
Takes flight, into the plainness of the air.

A piece used in your studio
  Where it frames the window
Lifting an eye to the sun.

There's something work makes plain,
   The point of rot being where you work
Clearing that out, to make small rooms of air.

The Grain Earth House on Mainland – it's on an industrial estate on the outskirts of Kirkwall, at the corner of Tuna Road and Swordfish Road, opposite Orkney Tool Hire and Andrew H. Wilson Electrical. As you approach you see a pregnant swelling in the ground and round it a metal fence. There is no one in attendance, no temple guardian from the heritage priesthood, and we lie sprawled on the thick resilient turf while Amanda fetches the key – you collect it from the Ortak Visitor Centre down the road and they give you a torch as well. We half walk half crawl down the tunnel to get inside. Once inside she switches off the torch and when I look back there's a slight twist to the passageway, but I can just make out a patch of grey light like a tongue reaching in from outside. Bumping into her I imagine a Marabar Caves scenario – but she's my wife, and there is no echo down here, just a steady uncomplaining silence. I feel surprisingly comfortable in here in the dark. Standing fully upright the top of my head just touches the roof, as if I fit inside. I watch a single drop of water as it gathers on the stone and fills, swelling slowly towards its final roundedness. It's all so firm and solid and there are no sharp angles or straight lines. No one knows quite what it was for – prehistoric re-birthing centre or simply somebody's larder? But when I get out and am walking back into town along the shore the land and its buildings have an insubstantial look to them.

That night I dreamed I was back in Hendon, standing at the end of the Vicarage garden. We moved there when I was nine. It was an enormous garden to find in a London suburb and when I look back it's as if I never quite knew what its limits were. In my dream I had come to the far end of it and I was standing there with a pack on my back watching a bird high up in a tree. The bird moved about as it sang and when it was caught in the evening (or was it early morning?) sunlight it looked itself like a drop of light. The noise it made was not a song exactly, more a sort of continuous, ecstatic trill and as it did so its body shivered. About the size of a starling, and with a slender slightly curved bill. Looking up at it I was filled with the most intense longing. I was partly a child, partly an adult – and these actually seemed to be two separate people standing beside one another. As I watched I was wondering, should I have come as far as this?

Hoy, 'High Island', is like an upgathering of darkness out there across the water. Is 'where I am' the wrong island? We'll take the ferry across.

A mountain is something to do, so we climbed Ward Hill, the highest point, piled a stone on the cairn to carry the lightness home, looked down to where the islands waited. It's the descent that makes me uneasy, that enormous downward swoop of hill. We set off, her in front. To our left there's a cleft in the hill, the course of a stream. It appears to be dry. Scrambling down there looks easier, or at least less worrying. I move across and start to make my way down. Recklessness overcomes me, I'm almost hurling myself down. Part of me is thinking, I ought to look back, make sure I'll be able to get back up if I can't go further. Now there's an even bigger drop ahead of me. I plunge forward and with a great yell I fall. I don't seem to be hurt but, getting up and looking back, I am stuck. I'm on a sort of wide shelf like a balcony and I'm not sure how I can get out at the side and back onto that worrying slope. There's a sort of pause. Am I going to have to be rescued? We passed some sort of mountain rescue place at the start of our walk. If they rescue you, do you have to pay? Going to the edge and peering round I can just make her out, sitting there reading her book. A comfortable, ordinary sort of afternoon. She comes over and I have another try. Although a strong walker I don't have much strength in my arms and shoulders. Finally under her coaxing direction I manage with a huge effort to pull myself out of there and back onto the slope of hill and half walking, half sliding I make my way down into the valley. This

cleft, the fall – birth canal? And then a competent woman comes and
with care and enormous patience she helps me out.

Next day at the Pow –
To sit here, look out from the same piece of land
As if being were a chair. It observes
Cormorant traffic all through the morning
And wonders, if I just lie here
What will visit me? So far
Two seals. My breathing vaguely hurts
On the left side where I fell.

It was the world broke my fall
Then threw me clear. On the beach at Rackwick
I lay next day like a partly broken thing.
In front of me a sea of restless jewels
Moved in among its flock of boulders,
Behind me smoke-smell in the bothy,
Its sleeping shelves, a frying pan hung on the wall.
I turn and watch you dive into the waves.
Four years ago I swam here too, can sometimes feel
The world will look after us,
Taking us in our fall.

Walking back alone,
Three pm, and the far hill's in sunlight.
Is there a moment of pure self?
Look back up the path, all or nothing –
The moment to throw it away
Where sunlight tenants the hill?
The looking part looks back at me.
Make everything familiar it grows more strange
And I was perched on the edge of something there,

The hill and me and something that made a third
Being that which I am lived by.
It closes the gap between *self* and *is*.
Something might open inside me, lifting the burden.
It makes me think of being indoors
In a kitchen, mid-afternoon
Where an elderly radio wanders over the waveband
And a clock is ticking the silence
As if there were an always-where-I-am
Something still as a lake in the mountains.
I stay in silence, the silence stays in me.

You can fly from Westray to Papay. It advertises itself as the 'shortest scheduled flight in the world' taking about five minutes. We went on the boat, which takes half an hour. The island is two miles long, and halfway up is The Knap of Howe, said to be 'the oldest house in Northern Europe.' The farm, called Holland, has been occupied by the same family for several generations. In one of the farm buildings they have made a museum. It's a heap of things, the labels like afterthoughts; skirt 'woven for a servant girl by her mother *ca* 1900', a beautiful thing, grey with one line of red near the hem; a 'murderer' – a long stone weight like something prehistoric, but with four hooks attached, for catching cod; a butter marker; a mourning brooch, a trivet. Mixed in with this are replicas of Pictish brooches and neck rings. There are farm implements and blowing in from outside the smell of silage and cattle. All unguarded and open to the touch Some knitted toys on sale 'on behalf of cancer research – please put money in the box'.

We went on down to the Knap: 'More recent excavations have shown that the Knap was in use between 3,700 and 3,100 BC. The two connected structures formed a dwelling house and a multipurpose workshop / barn. With walls still standing to a height of five feet the dwelling house . . . is reasonably spacious and divided into two living areas by large upright slabs. The outer chamber has a low stone bench running along the wall while excavations in the other chamber indicate that it was probably a kitchen of sorts with a central hearth and footings for wooden benches. The large stone quern, used for grinding barley, together with a smaller variant still lie where they were found all those years ago.' But the sea is much nearer now and looked at from above as you approach the house resembles a small fortress against the water just beyond it. You go inside and what would have been a short stretch of grassland, with dunes and the water beyond is now blue sea right up close, framed by the doorway with its massive lintel.

We walk on up to St Boniface, further along the coast. The chapel is a small stone box recently restored. We stay there reading stones. Then up to the main road, spine of the island, passing the airfield, stone field walls painted in broad strips of red and white to guide the planes. Over to the left is the Holm, an islet now with a chambered tomb visible as a low hump, and it all knits together. Hurrying back to the ferry a car stopped to give us a lift. He was going to pick up *his* house, he said. We stood on the quay and watched cars being unloaded, one with its driver and passenger – she was disabled – still on board as they swung high over our heads, and then the house came sailing through the air immediately above us, planks bundled together and carefully labelled, a house in kit form ready to be assembled like a child's toy, while patient cattle were waiting to be loaded, they too being crated and lifted through the air. So how did we get into this fix, moving all this stuff about? While he took photographs of the parts of his house sailing above us his wife explained, they would let it, and she thought it would be just the thing for someone to take on a long let, when writing a book perhaps.

Mainland to Westray – they were taking
The body across to the other island.
It was freshly prepared with flowers.

These are serious people –
There are carefully dressed old men,
With faces set like stone
And I feel like an intruder here
The poet cadging a lift on the hearse.
Someone has brought a baby, outspread
In its carry-cot like an opened shell
To cross sea's estranging mirror,
That teeming blankness. The hearse
Being unloaded now it sails through air.

The thing about islands is, there are always more,
Islands outnumbering islands – which one to choose?
One day whole islands might simply disappear
With their broken tombs, each a shadowy place for food
And soon we'll return to where the sculptor
Comes back each day from the shore.
We'll observe alterations in what he brings back –
He makes his own careful changes then sets the thing to rest.

Westray to Papay, moving from one to another
Increasingly you get an idea of land,
Something that tells us it thinks we are almost here.
It's the way each simply happens.
There's that island moment, a grating of keel on shingle
When, arriving, you notice how stone
Has made the light welcome.
Each lifts out of nowhere its
Gentle shock of arrival –
'I land you land we land'
Declension of pronouns in the morning sunshine
Then the way it blinks 'here',
Smells of silage and cattle

Breeze bending the grass, as it stirs
The dark red, small-belled fuchsia.

And so we left – it was only for a few hours.
Arriving at the pier the boat was already there.
I remembered how we'd arrived
At the Hostel on Westray two days before.
The place was open, there was nobody there.
We explored it waiting for someone else to arrive,
Visitor, caretaker, walking up the long hill?
But it was two after all who had landed safely there.

Opening

1
Cold spring, the light stuff stiffens,
Sperm drying on the leaflesss branch –
They're waking up. It's difficult,
The child so solemn, small and perfect –
A corpse is it, in the tent of her hands?

Rounding a corner of mist
The trees one mass of shadow
That'll glitter later, in
An afternooon I'm absent from   this
Being rooted elsewhere

'I remember I remember
The house where I was born'
It is an imagined structure
Buttressed against the dull air
Flags   litter   words – the semblance.

2
Wanting was in the mirror
Ahead there, where the crack
In its silver led me on

No longer shows me me
But seven years of wanting,
Seven times seven being
An age that I had come to
And saying 'I've walked my load'

What should I do with all that
Solitude   my mirror-walking
Since I have been set down
Here, at the table of plenty?

'If you were able simply
To be here you wouldn't need to come.'

On holiday aged fourteen
It was the first time I came
Sleeping in that four-
poster bed alone,
Where I fell off the cliff of myself –
The sweetness   it came
Like the waves' fetch
From such an enormous distance.

The next day was standing there
Her feet fringed with foam
Something vacant yet full,
So weightless its arrival
The way it opened into itself
And I was watching her   not so much
Desiring   as starting to recognise
My life has a sister –
In Autumn   when sunlight creeps
I'll take blood from those rays

Bits of it I could still catch
Where the breath turned home
And I am still writing this letter
Wanting to sing the world to rest.

3
Each step, a hopeful breeze
Tires, as if climbing
Staircase of air, the trodden leaf

Metallic blood-trace shining,
Desire   like an echo
Flavoured with smoke   a language
Whose cooling airs reach the concrete

Scandalous winds   it was
Like a cracked loaf
My bread of strangeness

The omnipresent secret sharer
Blunt-headed   phallic   serious
It faces the ache of a page.

So that I should be written out
On that irreducible membrane
The words on whose underside
Are parts of the secret letter
And birds are that other-
wise in air

Odd foreign stiffness of the
Press of feathers
So still and then
Abruptly fast.
One rattles in the vine.
It lifts a wing
Breeze stirs in ancient hair
The writing all takes flight, and
I'm deserted.

Today's uncertainty of blood
The haze of dried-out August grasses
Walking on down
To our river's green blooms

The poppy's seedcase, blackened, de-
hissant   it spits its distance.
Careless of the impulse
Each seed is an end of waste
And my face parched in a window's
Soundless black   cloud passing
Behind it somewhere's a
Faint mark I am and on another sky

But the blood was there before me
Coming   to its soft grave.
And next day over there she is
As if it's the one I was –

There's a quick fold in the sky
Bird enters, she guards her self with a smile
And all the ways in,
Forbidding hawk-profile

As if something has been growing
Inside me an otherness
Might step out to be given a name
You watching her that is I

The eyes half-closed in November sunshine
Can conjure such spaces
As if there had been two
Both of them me   and

One of them now, it's you – as if
It hears me, I'll lay down my load.

The opening section refers to the painting by Giovanni Bellini, 'The Madonna of the Meadow.'

Birth Right

1
Climbing the hill of our expectation
I survey the town,
Comb over remains, this Autumn of colours.

The Victorian suburb seethes with leaves
Where careful restoration
Is exercised on urn and cornice.

Painting them white I remember
How it might be again
When the page of our bodies

And all its
Dumbfounded writings
Are laid to one side.

Going past Clapton Pond in my progress
By the closed-up cinema, film scattered
Among broken glass across the pavement

The last vampire poster frays.
I walk past the Mothers Hospital.
The season has its requirements –

September, the plane-tree bark
Is flaking. You swell in our mirror
Already the same traverse

As twice before across expectation,
Auguries in your urine and blood.
The horn against the sunlight

This afternoon as I cross
From Walthamstow to Hackney.
The reservoirs' blank sheets

Of water are raked by sunlight.
Cormorants perched out on Heron Island
Dry outspread wings, in London's late afternoon.

2
Our city pegged out on its ground –
You are there, at the thickening centre
Where the bundle of waters has broken.

Now they have to keep changing the sheets
And testing – blood-pressure, temperature,
Dilaiton of the mouth of the cervix,

The foetal heartbeat. Outside
Some moisture collects in the sky
And a little white dust descends.

The ageing battery inside the radio
Keeps it chugging. The words climb like vapour.
The street is perfectly calm

And a woman beside you is saying
'Restrain the urge to push, you must
Breathe it out gently'.

A scream jumps out
From its terrible terminals,
Your head pressed alongside the wall

And the first cry issues,
Smoke that leaks from a statue, her
Head released from its origins.

Time's fall   of blood,
The wind still sealed with ice,
The afterbirth a quiet meat

And a turning away from inwardness
As the endlesly clever chain
Unfolds us its secret. And up it flies.

For Joachim

His brow being wounded by the laurel,
The Continental not the British kind –
Our vanity of cramped front gardens,
Ivy and holly that will outlast snow
As and when we have some.
Scylla, Medusa and Arachne –
Are these the names of girls? He wrote
I am my knot, my wound, my sore
And scared of the nocturnal monster,
Its horrible angry body,
Long beard and floating curls. The city
Collapsed into antiquity,
Dried out like porridge. He said
Herrings instead of ingots
I brought back, from my travels, enriched
Myself with boredom and old age.
Calm trains, well-lit, the aery
Underground, its gift of ozone
Are what we like. Our dogs
Grow lonely waiting for their masters.
Here at The Laurels we are more organized.
A black dog slavers rubies,
Fido he's called, has little close-set teeth.
She trails her coat
All the way from school
Dropping a scent – he said
A dried-up oak, old powdery honour
But what about posterity?
Old Roman palaces crumbled,
Refuge of a vicious heart. The bird
Kindles from its worm of fire,
The city opens like a book.

Joachim du Bellay: 16th Century French poet; lines in italic mimic passages from his 'Antiquitez de Rome' and his 'Regrets', two sonnet sequences.

Out

Out walking, to where this church
Lies stranded, like a cuttlefish bone
Near where a school of drinkers
Surrounds an eroded tomb.
Small fossils show through

In the sulphur-rich city air
Where stone is ground down to a dusty
Meal of light. In the sun
This darkening brickwork-province
Is ribbed like the intertidal

Sand on an afternoon beach.
Buddleia high on the station wall
Has fastened itself to the leagues of soot.
Inside, the small metal buttresses
Picked out in white are secular angels

And here are the timetables trains
Will seek to read their fate in.
A voice croaks over the intercom
As our carriage window produces
Its smoked glass effect.

The Orthodox is here too
Reading his Torah, where we've paused
At a vandal-proofed station set down
Like an emplacement
Of spears in alien territory.

On the far side, children are scholars
Of the word of the street and over
A table of shallow green a single
Alsatian is weaving his way.
Leaving the carriages' dawdling movement

I float down an avenue
Of lime and chestnut, and I am my own
Unique, solitary witness –
Such walking a kind of nostalgia,
Delight not weighted with meaning.

Nearby is a palace of windows.
He plays football with the Alsatian,
The dust-sheen on a broken window
Dull-shining, is like the hair
On the dog's arched back.

Me, I can take out a piece to label
As if it were something authentic –
It is hard to stay wordless.
Description, I'd say that it's like
Laying siege to an emptying fortress.

Let us consider, finally, the pedestrian. He scrambles across the city. The bits of it seem to consist of logical pathways, but nothing in the end quite fits together. He can see the joins, improvised-looking affairs, new concrete slotted awkwardly into old stone. Sometimes he feels the inside has been turned outside, and that is what he clambers over as he heads down unexpected tunnels, up walkways, following signs that leave him abruptly stranded on small concrete islands. From time to time he reaches something called a 'precinct', where other walkers awkwardly roam like an endangered species. "One day" he declares "you too shall rise above all this."

Whose life. Its story of emptying roads –
We have come here as for a
Curious kind of party, city abides
Its distance, the little deft knots of people

To consult
Appalling subways.
The footsteps measure
'Frequency of use'

In April, for instance, for-
sythia, tower block and one
Cloud, perched
On its shoulder. Below,
People walk in a powder of sunshine.
A foot's splayed under the arch
Like a fossil imprint
Set in the concrete.
Eight million lives awake
Exhaled as one, they have turned to the light
Feet set walking over
The same, ancient beaten ground.

The first straying band of light –
It seizes on a brain of song
Where birds are lettering the branch.
April. The bare earth
Is whitened and cracked by a drying wind,
The broken crystal scattered
Where wires above the rails pluck at the sky.
Streets end, a skylark rises
Ground mirrored in its song
Drinking at lunchtime
Coming out into autumn streets –
Let's go to the park .

Its hill slopes down to our river
And the scroll of an early sunset
Falls on the hours.

Keep starting to go back to it,
Lost haunt of a private beast
Pleading with every street round here,
Day's harmless blank I faded into.
Pale pink hydrangeas –
Colour emerges from their flattish buds.
It bleeds into flower, rhythm of process
Just as I am: dull roses
That hesitate in the wind,
A little rain on the lip of the street,
Now a musky smell of privet.

Under a grey arch of sky
Children flock. It's home time
While the heart shrinks to contrition
By delphinium's china blue.
Leaves rattle, as you pass
This day's dusty corner,
The playground being empty again. A life
Like a blade of grass is blown
Between palms, hums in the vacancy.
A jet trails blurs, and the
Shadowless voices of children
Bounce off buildings.
Last flowers have a special brightness,

Their stems grown brittle
With the first cold.

City of the warmed room –
It fills with anxious smiles.
Sun floods a wall outside

Where shadows arrive
As if from a great
Distance.

Long periods of idleness.
The iris for a theme.
Its heave, its muscle of root,
shouldering grey earth aside.
Emits such sturdy belts of leaf.
Now the petrol station's floodlit

And cars become more insistent on the hill. The butcher is sweeping up sawdust and blood. A side of meat sways behind him, returns to its numinous blood-ancient silence. A description of twilight, to include most of this. A street tips the people out. They are crossing the peaceful stones, ignoring this moment whose last bit of colour is going from the sky beyond. Is it something tipped out or tipped in? The lonely beach, a ribbed cloth of sand. The shellfish, roused by the brush of the tide as it returned, at evening extending the one foot swollen with blood that gripped the rock, goes foraging. Best to get out then, to try the city, its lip of darkness curled back, where seeds of light explode in dismissal. Some music in our roots. But look, it is already ancient with a little dust. Living somewhere quite different we hear but don't hear, following the evening – past the tobacconist and the stationer the quaint fish travels, between sun and moon.

GREETING WANT

Writing of artists, Rilke said
'Their lives have become atrophied, like an organ they no longer use.'

'It is delightful to be hidden but a disaster not to be found.'
D. W. Winnicott

Night Music

Traffic outside is a faint
Roar being poured into distance.
The road gleams under a streetlamp
Where the band of oil loosens and spreads.

Returning its rainbow stare
At midnight I have come back

To the quiet fossil burning
And the sloping desk of silence.

In Dalston

Buddleia whose musk
Is waste ground's tribute
Heralds street deals,

Goes brown at the edges,
Unreadable blossom slogan
Behind the Community Centre.

Such a degraded
Air the thin unstoppable
Branches contrive to feed on.

Such bricky text
Spells ruin in the mouth,
Such harsh leaf-clatter.

Taking Refuge

A curious dead August
Of city light
He teeters on his shadow
Is all but swallowed up

We can step into and out of
Our photograph of shadows
He has 'refugee status applied for'

What darker air still
Hides you in the sunlight brother?

Day upon day of late summer
Such a harsh depth of light
More and more of the
Dead leaves skitter about in it –

And our city, still hanging out
Its garment of frayed lawns
Cameras strung up in public spaces.

Stand and on one foot turn

The way light falls into silence

News Time

Some news on the point of the hour
That you walk past, going home –
A radio parked in the afternoon
That's overcast, then bright again

Where a hot cloud chases the sun
Past chestnut-castellations,
Then a yellow helicopter
In riots of the upper air

And how does the crime appear
From such an enormous distance?
The speck you are imagines the descent,
The fleeing grass, the silent upturned faces.

It quarters these quiet streets
Where patches of children dawdle
On the point of the hour.
They plot their next move

As they scatter across the system
In nineteen ninety. And now you are
This husk of meaning
That quietly sits at home.

White Lilac

White lilac, these restless nights
Whose heat disrupts the pages.

The nearly extinct are passing outside –
I must revert to these pages.

Reggae includes itself in the leaves.
The siren wails through my pages.

Brides of Babylon sway down the street,
Pass by in carriages of music.

In sweat-shops concealed behind
Derelict Georgian facades

The machines turn all night long.
Their finances enter the pages.

All this is a notion
White lilac has scattered.

Now the elderflower tips its plates towards you,
Its heavy must transgressed by traffic

Floats loose over city streets –
Tonight I will sleep in their pages.

For the Births

On the Suddenness of Signs
Every sign that I see
Seems to spread out, exfoliate.
In the same breath it blurs and flowers –

Engrossment by the air, the newborn
Baby, his lizard neck.
He sleeps in the crease of the hour.

The Swimmer
Our daughter dived up
Like a swimmer from the deep trough of blood.
You saw her in the mirror I held,
In the birth mirror such bloodstained sunrise.

A mild rain fell
Back on to exhausted streets, she lay
Her eyes feathered with sleep
In the arms of an explanation.

The Pear Tree

These blossoms, being about to open
Are scoured by spring winds –
I imagine the moment, count its heartbeat
Feeling the breeze on my unshaven face

Picturing the veil
The pear tree's petrified white.
There's dust beneath my tread,
An enormous silence holding back.

It is all potential
Disappearing into the act
And art is this counterfeit-fertile,
The lyric in its eyrie.

An aeroplane blends with the piano
Outside in the pleated air.
I ache to be crowned in secret.
Rejecting nourishment, I swell

Into heaviness, fingering the scales.
Against the ever-wakeful blue
The pear tree moves to its white
Heaving and thrashing, casting a litter

Of petals, incipient lushness,
Enough to fill those vacant afternoons
Where it and I
Embrace behind the veil.

This is the diurnal murmur
I wear my way towards
Till sound and hearing the sound are one.
Now it lights the midnight garden

And now behind the flying white
The leaves poke out like ears.
Meanwhile the carpet-veil of drifting
Petals calms. Oblivion

Will mend it when, unshaven, I'll
Enumerate each broken bud
Each time they break
Into our season of entertainment.

Voyage

We are beholden to those empty days
Through which our mission safely brought us,

Old maps showing islands, inky outlines
Wrinkled like an opening in flesh

And this one, with its own shy bird
There to be inventoried, perhaps extinguished.

Such tropic noons! We wipe the surface
Lifting the stylus: 'Heartwound'? Or 'Last Spring'?

We search the waveband where the police
Messages once stuttered. Now the music

Emerges to greet a freshly painted sunrise.
We're there! Palms waving over ocean . . .

That's where we'll picnic, on the island.
Its enormous ferns are all in fancy dress.

Somewhere inland and now protected
The small brown creature hides among the leaves,

Its voice one irritating note
Forever stitching up the breakers.

The Flaying of Marsyas
The painting by Titian

Now the aboriginal quarry
Has been strung up and silenced.

His pipes, just a touch of red,
Are tied to the tree with ribbon.

His flesh pours down like a river.
His eyes are blurred and distant.

Apollo's intimate attentions
Are lifting away the skin.

Nearby, some music is about to start.
The violin looks absurd

Though the singer's face is transfigured
Close by the bucket of blood

In here, in the gallery
All's won together in the paint,

A sticky urban night outside –
That other earlier voice

Being lost to streets and traffic.
A siren wails.

Days

Cloud pales to a softer grey
Then the light arrives, quite suddenly
At a window, here you are again –
Energy cancelling doubt
You confront an October townscape,
The recurring slight catastrophe of Autumn,
Raindrops' puzzling printout on the glass.
This net of nerves, these corrugations of flesh –
A body turns to yours in the mirror.
Parked cars look beached among the leaves.
Interior lighting is a shade theatrical.
Today the vacant sign –
You imagined its breath on your cheek
Where passers-by pause
On the edge of the flow, before disappearing
The season transformed
To a smell of smoke from a thousand gardens.

Waking and staying in
While the rain's sound thins, a radio blurs.
The lamp withdraws into daylight,
Our family exposed yet secret.
You are part of the same swarm
Chasing the features back
Into the mirror, trees
Flowing back to their roots
Out of a startled landscape.
Once a voice perched in there.
Each day now you'll see the street
Afresh, with a dull bemused wonder –
After so many years the lapsed
Trail of authorship's gone cold.

Camden Town Group –
On another day, the park
And, nearer, the pillar box
Partly obscured by one
Balcony railing, a red
Oblong smear with its bit of black
At the base, which is what
The mail van approaches at 4 p.m.
On a winter's day, 1912
Thirty years before I was born.
On an evening of muddy rose
And purplish trees, four passers-by
And the pressure of seeing
From the room half-imagined behind.
Its cruciform frame must have been
Like an ideogram of detachment.
From behind it he sought some tincture of life
In the muddy palette, looking out
Once again at those horrible, swirling skies.

YOU   that blend of
Vowels waiting outside
Time spills from like blood.
A patch of tree-bark's a mask of sunlight.
Some of it's used in each turning leaf,
Dissension at the centre, a line of
Breakage that radiates outward, language
Flutters, along the edge, "He
Wrote down everything he felt, beside
The silent grass, he looked for
A clue the twilight forfeits
In the distance of the sky, that
Terminal faint flush."

Next day, so much
Abandoned glory
Crossing a park of winter sunlight
In a flush of alcohol.
Street-alert children are wicked corpuscles.
The traffic gives off a brassy glare,
Is sluggish, as if
It were all one segmented creature
And the body, when you find it
After crossing half of the city
Will be marks on a canvas, and when you
Close in on it, quite roughly painted.
It is an execrable medium
Smeared on the once-billowing ground
Dyed with extracts of earth and rare metals.
The disturbing apparatus –
A brush filled with colour – continues to hover
Over her, each day each lung
Inherits some of the air
She once breathed in
Snorts sighs bellows and shrieks
Of all creatures that ever existed.
Caught in the act of looking
You sense in the picture's remoteness
Some residue of the human
As in a faintly disordered room,
Actaeon caught gazing at this diurnal shimmer
In the thicket of streets
Hunted by cars
Going out again, into the shudder of light.

Erasures

1
Still in flight, to shake oneself free
Of that thing, vista
Of absence, omnivorous reader.

Now the blood
Returns in its circuit, and now
After rain, the water

Is indigent among flagstones –
Comes sunlight
Like the cracked peace of a smile.

2
My neighbour's house sends songs
Of ash migrating
Across the Eastern suburbs.

Today, off Brick Lane, shadow's shifted
Round the sundial on a mosque,
First a church and then a synagogue.

Their factory squats in an eighteenth-
Century merchant's house. One day
A summons is pinned to her sari

Like a banknote to a bride
And they all decamp. Abruptly
Woodwork is treated, restored.

When you start the time is wrong.
Observe the 'heritage' –
Such abundance being shed, from distant dry hills.

This side of the rift
The broken clans are ornament
Where our negatives distil order.

3
With us the time is wrong.
It stays light late in the sky
All the way back from the airport.

Now distances whisper a greeting.
The evening primrose opens in its suburb.
A family's joined, from here to distant dry hills.

'Over there it's much better.
You really enjoy yourself.' At night
Fires of a wedding wind through the streets.

'At Shabrat the trees all pray'
Bending low to touch earth. Once a man
Woke and saw them and he was struck dead.

That night, you must fill a bath and look for
Your reflection by moonlight –
'If you can't find it you'll die.'

4
All round the town extend
Revisions of the landscape.
The fields of monoculture stretch.

This transverse slope of hillside's
Inflation-proof. To him
That hath it gathers

Slowly, with the various
Embroideries of word and token,
A durable feature

While waiting at the stairhead
Looking down over small, sleek gardens
And an unsplit bag of peat

You think about how she worries
(In the nicest and most tolerant way)
About her son's sexuality.

The digital clock on the telephone
Advances in tiny spasms. One day
This will have to peel back, and lift.

5
You read about jungles burning,
Ground cleared for ranchers. Today
First sun for ages is there in a gully of cloud

As you sit in the station
Bistro and scan
The impermeable typeface

Of a narrow plastic menu –
A 'hot chopped and shaped steak sandwich',
Plenty-in-absence sitting here calmly.

Mantle the flame, its
Soft pulsing flare.
The radiance startles.

Many look desolate, flowing past
Over a forecourt tricked out with steps.
Gusts of warm air from somewhere support them

In information city
Where leaf print-out fails at this season
And the starry circuitry, being limitless

Is replaced by the ordinary
Daylight of those who have
Bought themselves out of the town to its edge

To tend recent grass,
Being poured into air, into language
Hustled down the time-corridor

Those creatures and people still fleeing
As the ground is cleared and money
Is shifted around like a pulse.

6
Tired and ever more tired
An ex-imperial power
Sleeps and wakes and sleeps again.

The watcher incarnates his solitude
On the lip of morning astream with light.
Five cars stand round the holiday home.

He stumbles into the shore's half-circle.
Sun bounces off the sea in flames –
Exhausted fragments of the will.

Each sound of oyster-catcher, wave
Or gull's a gross intrusion
As he lies stretched back on the chilly sand

Eyes closed in half-sleep. His dreams
Rise and merge, take hold
With a kind of weary power.

7
Here's Europe, perfect early morning
And a fountain is wearing away the sunlight.
Pigeons explode in quiet squares.

There are smells of fresh coffee where daylight
Falls like an awning, across
The Cafe of the Four Winds.

Later that day you found it –
The Museum of Weaving, deserted and silent
Then went back to the street, a draught of sensation.

Now on a day in February
Another city, occluded by haze,
Bone-hard yet insubstantial

Which is yours by virtue of
The movement you make across it
Who have come to live at the fraying

Edge of a system. Close to extinction
Behaviours and languages flower.
In exile they train the vine

And still the partly-shielded walks in traffic
And still it dreams a life
Underwritten by landscape. There are

Such verbal shudders as night comes on.
The impotent quietist is roused at twilight
Being thus surrounded on the city's surface.

8
O my blessure! You are far away,
A bandit at the ear
Reading the book of energy, the book of light

Holding the silence as if with a switch.
A bird at the corner of vision
Darts round the edge of the planet.

Again and again
You wake up in the afternoon,
Another quietist at a desk

To listen to music, drink alcohol
Turning against
The blinding flare of hydrogen in the sky

Whence ducts convey these messages.
They pulse out clear down here
Into the new city

Organically bright.
Its air is charged with fine water.
Stars expend their residue of message

While blinking in libraries
Sit the hypothermic pensioners
Streaming out at closing time

From the brave municipal facades!
A daily tax on your strength, who still strive
To write down all you remember.

9
Do you see what I see –
Swifts crossing and crossing
Over the dry dusty garden,

Such endless disturbance
Of surface. They hiss.
You and I in our lives.

What do you do and what do you do?
You ride the descent
Up and about early

Moving into late summer,
The muggy blooms
Of inner-city weather.

There is this mounting
In the blood not early,
The 253 in Clapton Road –

Her braids like resin-sticky fronds.
Desires that weaken
Parabolas of motion. He

Dismounts his homage. There are
The timetables and small transactions.
There is that dusky sheen,

A bloom not rubbed off by the voyage.
Obligatory the descent
Of certain juices and a private musk,

A part of the world, ours, held
Just before exploding
Into the dense heart of the local star.

Coda: In These Last Days
It was planned as a story of prolongation –
Prolonging the note, the hour, the orgasm
Buying art books as a secret consolation.

He admired the city and its tainted prowess,
All the particulars housed in there,
A mirror bulging with fruit, the table

And on it a breakfast, expertly
Choreographed. But an unfinished work
Is still more use, and he rose into air

While the day lay abandoned biting its fingernails
And the novel dozed in the suburb's pages.
In the shining kitchen she began to cook.

He could see all this, cruising above
At a faithful altitude. She slit the bulb
As per instructions carefully propped.

Her small knife went to the root of the matter.
Heat and oil accomplished transformations.
Still he quits the replete page,
                              goes higher and higher.

Section 2: the opening stanza is adapted from a passage in the nineteenth-century Urdu poet Ghalib's prose work 'Dastanbuy' ('A Posy of Flowers') which contains a description of the sack of Delhi by the British at the time of the Great Revolt in 1857.

Section 3: Shabrat is a Moslem festival, sometimes celebrated with fireworks; it recalls the 'Lailat ul Qadr', the Night of Power, when the Angel Gabriel first revealed the Koran to the Prophet. The 'distant dry hills' refer to the region of Pakistan from which the child's family may be presumed to come.

Seven Dawns

1
Dawn breeze was
Shaking a fringe of leaves
Just the outermost ones
At the tips of branches.

First signs – a bulb grown pale, in
Someone's sleepless window

That absolute sense of expectation

Who talked who brought the light
And afterwards there was
A kind of lofty silence

2
As if there were some lifting
Where light bleeds in. It grows
Quite pale with birdsong

A page's corner, my life
Turned over then
To be examined. Strange

It crowned. In
Crept the day
And flattened itself on the boards

Beneath the door
One page of light like the rasp
Of an animal tongue

Something I missed
Was absorbed there

As I went out into
This blurring effect of the light

3
Possible too this sky
That creeps into bed beside us

Day breaks on the stairs
The cat brings the sky in her mouth –
A broken bird held sideways

Waking to this foreign light
There's safety all around me
My own name knocks at the door

4
One leaf, an ear
Its growing is
A silence in the blood

Night died with its scents in my arms
Daybreak: the same bird always
Utters, I answer, look –

The sky is only made of
Air and broken writing
Reach to the other

Transcending nightmare
To be here where
The birds are, in the safety of the air

5
Erotic, to
Join sky and now

You, winged pronoun, spinning down

Ground open wide
To imagine the other

He woke and stepped down
From the platform of sleep

One silent sky
One absent chorus

6
A chill May dawn, and still
The taint of last night's

Woodsmoke   bed of ash
The dove-grey flakes
Like serpent stirring
A little coil, will
Eyes blink open?

Move soundlessly as I can
The door an enormous leaf
And into the creak of day

Now, listen

7
One hour after dawn
The ruined barn: stone blush
It matches the red earth

All the things still here
I wake up for
Hey! That's my snake.

You are sufficiently "you"
In a domestic charnel house
Of crayons and soft toys.

Down here on the Farm
It's like a children's story.
'The Famous Five on Holiday'.

Coda: Down There
Walking over the fields
In the blue-grey noon grown warm
The folds of your dress
Abandoned stone barns
Children dawdled in the hedgerow
The sky was as faint as a veil
In front of a ruined cottage
Southernwood glistened, the
Acrid smell of its crushed
Leaves. On a roof rusty iron
Lifting an ear to listen –

I went off and came back
It took years
But they were still there

Sunning themselves and
Keeping their distance

I concealed
My messages
Till they died

And now we sit round a table
Five who escaped the disaster
Congratulating each other
The way that families do.

We lie, two abandoned statues
Growing chill on the surface
Smoothing the bed
Turning a page –

But here we are, in a moment
Of self-conscious quiet
Succeding the music

Iris

My huge own darkness –

I want to have my say

Rodin's 'Head of Iris': the staring eye-sockets are two pits of grief and anger; a lopsided, indeterminate mouth. From the back the head is like soft dough, yet the overall effect is so massive and powerful, the face set in implacable, reined-in rage, but at the same time looking as if it might at any moment break up into tears. The planes and facets of the sculpture are, like the mouth, all slewed round so that one cheek is a bit higher than the other. The longer I look at it, the more it withdraws into enigma.

Iris, who carried messages, and that was all she did.

Is it you, or is it her?

Dead words on a page; a necklace of stings.

The 'not impossible she'
She is garlanded like a title page

I'm in her sky or I am nowhere
I have come back as a cloud of absence
Seeking and refusing closeness. A curious kind of
Hunger, this – to be seen

Such as will not be calmed
Obdurate as this sunlight

Is, falling cold
On to afternoon pavement

I want you here and do not want you
Except in such a distance.

I rest in my darkness
Is your message, I came
Through traffic to reach here
And stale air, you
Squat in your head
Beside a blank river.

Sibyl vain
Prophetic leaf
 I
  chew
Whose bitter
Taste of seeing

The brain-stuff: water clanks
Clear in a bucket
Chill weight of it

Shakes up the light. Her call is to emptiness now; how the dark tends towards me! Childhood, a kitchen of cupboards. So, fly in through every door.

I could invent tears. What I see in me, not becoming, back there and Iris coming to rest inside, a bird on each dark shelf. Messenger-flight back inwards. Sky shines with her absence.

Now, Iris, this bulky head, this moulded lump of darkness. The deep eye-clefts. She had a little crooked mouth to drink with

the grip, rhythm-steps

That was enough! I said, and flew back.

What's missing, it's in the mouth, all you can tell. Where the sacred smears its blood in ambiguous power.

Pepper blood taste. The mouth roof lifts. Come down with me now, to the sea-cave, the gallery shore. Its floor is covered with dead leaves.
What times we had in my imagined, dusty studio! Adolescent, in an afternoon of wrecked statues, all that was left to me, and the sea through a window – or was it painted on canvas? Now, walking outside the enclosure, the heart's radical, outside the silence I'd invented, is it nostalgia, for the almost-real, the life I had never had?

Then back, to the mirror's silvered zero.

I am circulating the gallery in a walkman-twitter, abstractedly staring at the almost real hung on the wall.

Iris, dumpy bird, I plead you back, back to my shelf of darkness; to this useless studio, my delicate predator –

What my lips tug vainly at

"Yet her low twitter had more charm
Than any full-mouthed song."

The seamstress of light
Today, cold spring

Is wind under the heel
Tourbillon of rubbish

Is not re-
Cycled in an air

Lofty of purpose but is caught
Quite high up in the trees

A plastic bag that will fade
Over months of an urban summer

Whose nights are a fabulous
Inheritance of dew

Today the light digit carrier
Passes over my bright rubble

At the checkout, walking the measure
Of black coded lines to a heart-count

Such as, markings
On a bird's wing

Where it flies up, messenger coasting
Down past the violent signs

At the checkout walking the measure
Of the glass's edge of fracture

Light striding to dance
Quite pointlessly on the diamond

Where you aren't, reaching in
Past nowhere –

What glass defends
From touch

It's an accident in the mirror again
And another bite at the laurel's
Doubtful crown.

You, as a split in the narrative
Are where the book falls open

While 'I' divides the dream
'You' turned round, turned into 'I'

Desire: its vertigo
And will learn how to take the bright couple into us.

But Iris you only carried
Messages, from
Parent god to parent god

So I remember it too
From one to another flying
And not knowing myself at all

And so like that
And in spite of it, I
Announced it then –

Once we were alive and now we sing.

The rocking together
Look past her shoulder
At what streams away from us

See! she has only one sandal

The artist insists
But they don't know what to do
With this indecent gift

Her open thighs
The distance in between
It cries and sings

The mouth   warm   inward cave
Speech   not penetration
From no more than a child
Each moist syllable formed
Out of her separate anger
She is all covered

The lightword sperm
Stream of particles
And the receiving power
Screen angel and the
Iris-cursor winking

There is that
Something high
Annunciation

Unwinking the mirror's siege

To let me be
Tender towards

There is a life
That leaves no mark
It left me singing in that tree

Who is the unknown Other everywhere.

Rodin's 'Head of Iris' is in Tate Modern. The two lines beginning 'Yet her low twitter' are from a poem by W.H.Davies.

Bird Talk

As I came out from the stone house at twilight, it rose up by the field's corner, brown-barred, pale on the underparts, the sudden plumage an absence again where it skimmed away low over long grass, unidentified. I remembered the faint persistent call that you heard at the edge of another field – some rarity – and how you waited all through that evening and the next, hoping it would come again, held between excitement and disappointment.

The watcher walks on the hill. You can see him take out binoculars, notebook, to people emptiness – so what did you see out in those quiet fields? And what do you remember? In a ruined house that we passed on the headland the shadows played with sunlight. A far sea crawled across the empty doorways. The dusty hardened track, spots of rain in the air, late summer flowers, scabious and toadflax, colours so much fainter but clearer than the garden kind, where they bleed out at the edges of pesticide-purged fields.

Released from my page I recall the markings and try to conceive the bird. It is big with silence, uniting softness and strength. Absent risen dream returning to its place by the gate it coasts silently down, to the place I can almost remember.

There is a painting of a girl on the wall of the studio, head and breasts, the top of the picture cropped very close. The girl has her head tilted a little back and to one side, her mouth drawn open in a scream. Two further canvases are placed one on each side, part of the same work – two swans.

She opens the drawers of her plan-chest; sheaves of drawings. Work, the deliberateness, the calmness of it.

She is painting black swans. She's Australian. She goes to Regent's Park – there are two on the lake there. Doing this regularly, she becomes aware of other regulars there, bird-obsessives.

The otherness of birds, she says, their ungraspable quality, the way you can never quite get close. Antipodean, impossible, reversed colour. But she refuses explanations of this image. It floats, simply, on the canvas, dives in and out of it with folded wings. She has notebooks filled with them. They become like calligraphy.

These necks veering away and coming back at you, and the extraordinary pointed knob of red, a single gesture of paint, for the beak. The neck in this one is more than ever like a snake. Sometimes male and female seem to be remembered being united in that otherness.

The water is the page, where one comes to rest on the magnificence of the paper. Looking at the girl again, at her open mouth, quite small and pointed, and suddenly you see it is just like a beak. Beak-scream the voice at last descending into –

Bird Talk

Blow on the name
Watch it sprout feathers

Blow on the clock face
The numbers catch fire

Here is the child half-
Starved with waiting

Last night my father came back
Sour breath and stubble chin
The slack skin living and warm.
We embraced
But he was too near by far,
A man of sorrows and of silence

I was with him in the hour
The darkness still
Not bothering to fade.

The paper now: loud thorns,
Small voices that poke through, bird music.

Deep aboriginal sadness
Of the child skulking
At the door of his father's study

Meat against sunset
Sky drained then flooded.
What is it that's walking about up there?

Years later I think, looking up at the sky
And I am rebuffed by its empty dazzle.

The tears all dried up
The bowl cracked and dry –

Always such turning away
One from another, into
Such careful
Solitudes
    always.

Down here, paternal shades –
I am beating the bounds of memory
Odd noise the rain is making
On leaves, the way the birds sing through it.
Null blossom, borrowed laughter.
My father large and absent after his stroke.
Going out today I wear his scarf, his coat –
My hands across the keys
The tune is somewhere else.

The gyroscope I played with
Rocked gently on its point of balance
It seemed to defeat the world, until it fell.
The prism sent a flare
Of colours onto the wall –
For ages playing with sunlight
First thing on summer mornings, in the empty classroom.
Later escaped into libraries
And their long ache of afternoon sunlight.

I've had enough
Don't ask me what of
(Enough is too much)

Have made peace
(As if war cared)

And I am the unsolved residue.

Day ends outside, not rightly understood
There's sunlight still on the cornice

Rose hammered glow
Up in the thought
Of a sky where it flies

The portrait photographs faded
Into the well of the stairs

I cradle the cup in my hands
I've joined these others here

And am among them
Silent as
A column's fluted eye.

My petals of anger
Were torn away silently –

Untying untying
They had come with such capable fingers.

I imagined swan-talk instead
On afternoon's mirror inverted

An early sky upbraided
By its scattering of birds.

But those monitory birds fell like cinders
I was swallowing, swallowing

And today a dulled eye of wine
Sits slumped in the glass.

The sky has burned down
To an ash, is inside me

The head was served last
On its plate of shadow.

My birds in the dream I wrote down
Were amazing in their paired flight

Rising up in the call of a bird
Were the feelings that could not be named.

The banished child has come back now
An ungrateful bringer of news

Encounters the braille
Epiphany of another's flesh.

Now by this contagion –
The season's branches budding

And notwithstanding dragons'
Teeth that were sown in that suburb

I walk up the road once again
Being talked from the site of absence.

The food groans on my father's table
I am marooned on the threshold

Approaching the table I reach
Out as it bursts into flame –

He is in starlight in rain in the grove
I bring him the dreams as offerings

And if you only knew
Each moment of light on the branch

Is the prodigal returning always
Who comes back to a burning house.

How little the noise our parents'
Lives made, sunlight fading a carpet

But to read myself there before I was,
Out of old letters, to watch them come closer!

Owning the moment, still
Carefully guarding these papers.

You sent me away I'll not tell
How in secret now I am sharing you

The two of you who colluded
I'll circle around you

Weaving you stealthily
Out of my anger now.

From the root like a thumb, blunt capital
Letter, a name it begins

Two coming together always
In the arbitrary knot that we practise

Inside someone else's flesh.
Each act of it is a supple

Display in front of the dead.
Years on, if we could only

Find ways to get the distance right
You and me who each are walking

In front of this panel of glass
In many different guises.

Pieces of shrapnel, a billowing
Parachute stuffed in her bureau

Gas mask still hanging behind a door
And the rolled up black-out curtains . . .

Photographs kept in the dark
Of a drawer were brief tokens of light

Each shiny unbroken skin
Not quite telling how we survived.

Twilit soaked gardens, one summer
Evening, the downpour ending

In a faint smoke I go out walking
This singing light like a wound

Where one bird raises
Its unelected voice.

Shades

Feet crackled over
A text of old leaves
Beneath the branches
Further and further
Into a screen the
Cold clouds, with its breath.
Tomb airs. I
Hesitate like the child
Who once floated over
A darkened landing
Hand on the knob
Of freezing brass,
Waits, hearing a certain
Kind of movement.
But sunlight comes, warms
Will bruise a white lawn.
And swan labours on
Into a headwind
In a creak of pinions.
My Handbook of British
Birds by my bed
In search of the sign –
Elusive, it ran
Over the page –
Today I am crossing t
The marsh, the reeds
Beaten down under ice
And remember
The dancers' smiles
In the painting, who move
On a wintry sky
Where the leafless
Sapling bends
To the steady music
And thinking how quiet

On the floor of his
Dressing room, I would be
Watching him shave,
The cut-throat razor
He always used
That I still have
In a drawer somewhere
And the toilet-case made of
Leather, the things that
Fit in compartments.
I pack and unpack it.
I've found I can fly,
Clutching my wood
Aeroplane to float
Down the stairs and outside.

Today what I am
Will bravely ride out
The afternoon's frozen
Sunshine whose hollows
Get covered with writing.
Innocent pleasures –
The mouth in the sky
At play in the world.
But I have a small
Song in my head,
A taste of ruin.
I do not want
To get too close
Lest I become careless.
Once when we rose
At daybreak, ours
It was, whitened grass
Atomic trinity.
Ice that the children

Have broken refracts
In points that I stare at –
Which one is me?
But the moment unread
Sinks back in the blaze,
Cars blink their lights
A useless knowledge.
Inhale smoky twilight –
The wound is memory
Silent invisible.
I stop and I pause
In front of what I'm
About to explain –

Father, the shadow
Over frightened grass.
He is just ahead
As I leave the gallery –
Baker Street, Marylebone –
He disappears under
The wheels of the cars.
As I rejoin
The chain of lights
Remains of the city
Shine by his side.

LAUREL

Laurel that grows
In suburban gardens
Along with the lanky
And dull-leafed lilac,
Both shrubs that will thrive
In fumes of traffic

And Daphne – who maybe
Was always laurel. Not snatched
Into a cleft in the earth
She was simply there and not-there.
'It's how I am', and he was
Left wondering.

One grew in front of the Vicarage –
Its berries the colour of lipstick
Such as they used to wear then.
You could write on the back of those leaves
Using a sharp piece of twig –
It was all part of feeling closer

Because so much smaller then
To that shrubbery smell, dusty and acrid,
And the broken wood's faint scent.
Of such sensations you're made
And it was a comfort then
Being merely you in such moments

To watch them from your quiet distance
Where they colluded like gods.
It was my anger they frowned on
It smoked like a sacrifice. From such
Burnt offerings each
Turned away.

One day, I can remember
I looked round from where I was playing.
Something was in my hand
I threw it, the window smashed.
She was standing right behind it
Yet all that I can remember

Rooted to the spot like that
Is her, not even angry, saying
'You might have hurt me'
And I think, she must be still indoors
Somewhere inscrutably busy.
On the back you could scratch your message

Scoring the underside's dull film
And I am the child still out there
Watching the speckled leaf, one
Single remaining berry
Bright red, long-lasting, the one
My parents had warned me against.

Found

Hearing the owl in the city –
Who'll whistle up
My fruit of solace?
How far is it
From here to his small heart?

Up here I'm
Late on a hot night
Someone just pushed up a window,
A fork on a plate, such
Singleness of sound.

Not being found –
And if I had that voice
A stairway to climb
Up and down, down and up
To the slaughtering ground,

Again the owl's call floating in
So hasten to that voice
Turning archaeologist.
It's in me but it
Speaks to me from somewhere else,

The other, that I
Felt for in the night,
Too far and much too near –
My strangeness
And a cold breath coming into me.

Building and building
A lonely maze
I'm waiting, end of summer
As a garden waited for the child
Being separate, out there, still not found

And so it was I came back, found you
Stupid with sleep, the light still on,
And the curtains not quite shut
But parted like blank lips
Half open onto the hot street –

One day I said I'll tell you all about it.

The Vine

These nights alone, being strange,
But to each day its task.
I drill in locks that wound the wood

Around the window frame –
Outside, the chopped-back vine has flourished
And the tendrils' frail persistence

Goes reaching through the air.
So many cries being taken down
To feed the root of it.

The broad leaves multiply
Crowding the light, and hiding
Small, unripe berries

Pale green like sea-glass,
With a bloom on them
As if someone had breathed there.

Last year birds struggled in there.
The concrete underneath
Got spattered in lime-tinged purple,

The shat-out skins like word husks
And those faint berries half-remembered,
How each its perfect music held.

November came, blind light
Furrowing the dark
The final bird had flown,

Escaping like the print of light
Day briefly emptied onto brick
Against which the stripped branches hung.

Its Radiance
Something that does not know us: but that we are known by

Its radiance
       sent part of you to sleep.
You woke beside this other.
Separately each breathes. Light rises, falls.

Hydrangea near the sea-shore's speckled pink.
Sunlight and wind comb the tamarisk over the rock
Whose turning edge will lift us into time –

A piece broke off and weathered.
We're in the gap that opens out,
Blood-berries, on a white sky.

Rain blowing in the wind, the track still dry.
The words are in a shallow grave
But we can hear the sea together.

Between us the stone set wandering –
Disturb the grey chips and send them skimming,
Wait for the sea to return.

Pebble, roof of the mouth
Is lonely as the salt
On its cold forehead.

There is another book, one we sit reading
All afternoon, beside the sealed-up well.
The silent trumpet-flowers. It's overcast and still

On a day the ants take flight.
They're covering the path, a living veil.
If I were asked to name you what could I say?

Going back the way I came, eating the path up
Nightfall, dew and its million forms of stillness.
These bring me to the room of you, blood-wine.

Was it us or the words?
Sun glinting
On the glass-fronted bookcase

We were halfway between
The life and the book
Neither real nor unreal
Dust suspended in sunlight

Puffed up as the pages
Closed. Then a flutter
Of leaflight above my desk.
The garden filled up with wings

In the gradation of afternoon
Striped with hours like the tiger
In the theatre of wrecked flowers
In water the branch reared back from . . .

I opened the door
The words got there first
Making it ready –

A book that's been
Lifted up in my name

Over a stile of words
I have come

To show you ourselves in the painting
So each falls in with each
What cried us in the wood
Is now a varnished god

We uncover ourselves
Laying aside the folds

Step naked into the pool
The painting holds its breath

Standing in front of the picture
The watcher's thumbprint's on the glass

Or pause in the country of titles
'Dogs and dead game at a fountain'

The fruit splits with ripening seed
'Halt during the chase'

Here, minds enlarge the hour
Quietly one takes

The arrow from the other's side
'Journey to the interior'

Silence like a token
Is pressed against our lips

On our way to the listening country

Curtains blew inward
As pages of air
Passed over our bodies
Moistened with secrets

Then each said, to speak of
The picture we hide in
Here and there pointed out
Whose head is it hangs

Monstrous again, in the
Mirror of pronouns?
Not knowing where it
Belongs, so to speak

From another room, those voices
The way they fit together
Seamlessly. I want to speak
                The table
Is loaded with all the words
Of her, and her
         Dumb other wanting
To be the firm tongue, inside one,
Abrupt speech, remember
How the truth came in spurts

I peel myself in dreams. Next day
That sheen of absence
Word litter, leaf litter

Remember from how far back
And near, the changeling
Girl boy girl
Watched and waited without hope
Enormous sunlit Autumn stillness
All the years of waiting
Till the years fail me hurrying here
Still I imagine
How they will feed from my hand

Remember, generations
In the windless orchard
She spreads the cloth

As they unpick their marriage
To live out what remains,
Fall between memory and desire

Day by day the transformations of sunlight
Are carried into the timber, the starch of heartwood

Waiting under the tree there
To be this husband/wife

What she said
What my mother saw
She never told me

Knowing myself before,
Myself I banished
Who'd never sought to please

She sent me out there
Wearing the right clothes
Another face was hanging in the mirror

    Years later
I made love to myself
In front of the painting I'd made

Between cold legends
I made a birth

All this was in the plan
The hour of flight, and every
Detail

Flight disguised
As ceremonial

He slipped through my hands
Just as I slipped through his
Landing in a spray of moments
She said –

I'm on the outside calling him
And he's on the inside calling –
I'll go away and be his page of secrets

Turned wholly away from the act
His gaze was the shadow –
She was translated
Into the song of a bird

It was just as it was
Darting in out of the wood
Over the window-seat, its embroidered cushions,
Her scream stitched in
Dozing beside the open window
He sat, waiting for what would come
The voice to return to itself
In unbelief
She would return
Swooping and diving in

She ascended, descended
The scale of difference
And how they wept –
Between them there was the breach
Of blood, this stinking ditch

To be sung in the early part of the night

Dewfall feels the ground
As cold as metal
October morning
That haze and slight moistness
In the late heat the insects wake up
Trees blur on the hill
From a distance almost like friends
And swearing eternal bonds
Each from the other receding
Who will not return again
To the promise not kept in the mist

As the sun begins to go down
To light the underside of clouds
As shadows deepen in trampled sand
And the egg-sac sings in the light
She draws her cardigan round her
Stares past her children
Playing at the waves' edge
The sky blue behind her
The sand sings in each grain
Her presence blends into her absence
She falls into
The great gulf of light

Begun in secrecy, still not concluded
They were not fiction and they were not fact
In silence and in longing
Who wavered together like an invisible flame.

Outside the night did clever things with darkness
The wind got silly in the trees
Lamplight fell on their life
Now close the book she said, enough of that.

After making the love they made
And they were not even born
He lay there curled up in the afternoon
As if safe inside the book's pages.

Trying to forget where he was
He waited around, it got colder
She met him on the edge of the day
She held her face up to his like a mirror.

She nurtured him
Inside and outside and inside again
They were not quite the same, swam
Upwards together to the door of air.

He was saying, look, I've come back
Walking past the white flowers
With the hill and its trees behind him.
She was eating the path with her smiles.

But he wants someone new he can show himself to
He looks past her into the mirror
Where they're sleeping
He says, I will write it and leave it here –

The piece of me I almost held
For those who have eaten the fruit and are separate
Into the wind she leans with the children
He stays, wonders where the blood goes.

It is afternoon and she hasn't come back
Air's heavy with her absence
Where he sits reading the book that's been left
Beside the unguarded well.

And the other, the one
We both reach out for
A border of limbs

Is warm
Rush of speech
In clouded flight

What is s/he like?
Laid together the limbs
Together
Ease us back into the dazzle –

Returning to one alone
Turn aside to write this down
Always this supple practice
Who speak in warmer accents
On a day when the air is ours
Here and the one beside her

And afterwards
      Leaning over, you
Poor forked
      Lightning in my arms

In the act's final shudder
A moment of blankness, something strange
Between living and dying
What's born has died so many times
Out of its egg the serpent weaves

And a rising warmth disturbs,
An embarrassment of blood

Where, grounded in one another
We shall inhabit ourselves
Outside rain freckled the still pond

Imagined –
The play of bodies and light, unendingly

An experience of loss we're the site of
Being born with us in the world
But we fill this place
As completely as any other
Day by day we approach it
With emptier hands

Knowing you like this the world
Changes more visibly
Its impermanence made fast to your heel
Stealthily the hills are fading
Time will complete itself without us
This time round while together
We complete the study of each other's helplessness
On the edge of uncertain weather

Leaving the beach
We walk up a narrow valley
Past where the hives are
Sunning themselves by the wood

Then look back – the living branches
Sway against distant water
Breeze in here, ocean-quiet.
From a hill of patient voices

We walk the island's tracks
Past their dust-whitened verges.
Round our house the leaves
Practise an absolute stillness.

The afternoon seems shamming dead.
Each thinks, to lie in there

Abolish difference for an hour
And we would be neighbour to that stillness,

Sweat drying, the smell of hair.
Today around the headland
The sea is talking like
A voice in someone else's ear.

In the train I'm passing
An asphalt-dark playground
Emptied of its tuneless voices

The seat beside me
Is hot with late September sunshine

Outside the dawdling carriage
Michaelmas daisies run wild
Reverting, over waste ground

To the usual colour, the
Muted purples,
Whose vigorous striving
Will fill the surrounding air with seed

The rosy shellfish-coral

Mothers up its blood

Half in fright and half adoring

Laila

Laila sucked my brother's cock, the slag

Inscribed on a desk: here I
Paused watching clouds
From an East London classroom –

Trapped energies that might
Be freed, into
Laila! – this sense of play.

The countryside is full of bits.
What's that the dog's got
Tossing it up in the air?

An active watching
Where swallow is riding the corn in the wind.
Our bodies come unglued.

Pigs blunder nimbly
Up there in the wood.
Life is just far enough away.

Last night I dreamed a girl
Gave me a red flower,
Her own wise blood. Today

Our weather, the dragon's tail
It offers us its portent
Seeded with flying drops.

A dusting of rain
Falls on red earth that's
Hard as iron.

Afternoon silence
And here are the single
Sounds to talk me home,

Stone wind dust
The animals are sly
Silk limb screen.

Sensing the bird at my shoulder
Among such low close hills,
So much fertility –

Herefordshire's red earth,
Faint rainwet scent of honeysuckle.
That other odour moves

Towards a conquest of the noon
Spreadeagled in the serpent's bower.
So the wind dies

Down on a low green stone
In homage.
My ally, how the juices ran!

In a far corner
Of the graveyard
Behind massed undergrowth

Is water that runs clear.
Hear the rain now plead
Its curtains in the air.

I write my words all over, make
A screen of joined-up writing
Being there but not-there

Where I am still and always
As the lyric spurts its distance
And falls back to the ground.

It starts in imitation
And looks around for rivals.
I am being written against!

Swifts zeroing in and away
Take shelter in
The margin of the descriptive.

But I'm still pressing on
Back to that landscape's
Lanes, its endstopped valleys.

And so am being sailed
Wisely to that coast of blood,
Protracted labial gaze,

At daybreak come outside alone
The birds all singing surely
More than they need to,

Fingernail moon, a whirr
Of wings, the teasing flock,
Its aerial clockwork –

A child once moved
Like this in amazement
Through the chorus of unknown names

And ways of longing changed the air.
Now I'll follow where
The red thread runs across the contours

Over our map's shallow folds.
And the wild geranium,
Garden escape, you levered

Carefully out of its hedgerow –
We carried it back home
Where it took root, such a fine

Purple line like contours
Being traced
       on every petal.

Glyph

    A   E

         A

    E   A

The day: pressed up close
To it, face to the glass,
The bird claw prints are
Cuneiform tales, a
Baked message.

But scribe-acts by writing-light
Are a silence that swells inside me.
There is an idea of the south,
Stone that waits to be pressed,
And under the south

Slippage –
The cuneiform tablet
Is inside a clay envelope
That carries the same inscription,
Sits under the stone of my tongue.

So saying, she handed me
Another pair of eyes –

It was someone who'd wept at my shoulder.
Now carrying on from there
I'll tell my story

The moment I drew breath
Being knowledge, light, estrangement.
I never quite got over it.
I should like to lead my life
Unreadably just the same,

To drink from the lake of memory,
A very pure fish its syllable
Quite unknown elsewhere.
Coming from those depths
One such braves a standard

Today being
A fish head at the back door.
Tench. He surfaced one final time.
Later I find some more of him,
Body of browns and greens

Glitters
In colours of Autumn.
The cat spews some up in the bathroom.
The emptied pond stares upward.
Our air is visited by wings.

Apollo going out of doors
Is treading down feathers,

Important ghosts and sunsets.
She crosses the room to me
With her word in her mouth.

But being so
Filled with the unspoken
I'm only partly here –
The crime-text, me,
Escapes out into walking

And temperature sings in the air,
An art emotion rising
Between feeling and intellect
Under that Gorgon-aegis
Where everything has a name.

Echo of something
Something I can't quite name.
My statement, in the interim,
Leaves me behind
Its print at daybreak.

Star writ wet bill,
Siren lens,
Serenades, a new kind of music
As if you went out with
One pocket too few

Glorious with hunger
And there were two distinct wounds.

Getting it in the neck
Here in the city: her fresh sweat smell
An estuary's marine tidings.

The cloth dries stiff as card.
The distant architecture
Breathed in is a promise
At the horizon's gate
And the light has come to find us.

I move into the space of it,
My hollow in the air
The self is learning to inhabit.
Seeking itself to please
It is slight lyric in its purse of moments.

October, shrinking apple
Imprisoning its juices
Near traffic, the heavy swarm –
And there is, that I might be more
Comfortably dumb,

A large wind to guide my hand
Here to the small page
I always sidling off,
A water-drop over glass
In a museum of light.

I yearn towards those objects
Alarmed in their bright cases.

I thought, perhaps if I
Keep still as that
Someone will come and find me?

The afternoon goes past
Looking at scripts it cannot read –
In a bowl the letters sit.
But give me the earth's
Reflection on that bottle's shoulder!

The light being there an arrow,
My tenses hung out to dry.
The search lies fallow.
I've carried on like this
For many years.

The slightest mark still fascinates
Touches on meaning at every point,
The light-hold a long way off.
The hinge of sunset,
False door I pass at will,

Now going outside. The one who will be

There is there already

'*Aeaea*: A surname of Circe . . . hence magic arts are called *Aeaea artes* or *Aeaea carminae.*' Smith's Classical Dictionary

Poor

Mouth-hunger

   anger

Go out and get some

And write some

Filling the space

The space that opens
In my solar plexus
Take it out new for you

Is this, a book of stairs I climb

Mouth on top of a sort of stem
Out in it
Alcohol afternoon misery

Sluiced with cold
Buckets of sunlight

But O to be just where I am
And comfortable in my skin
The light a sufficient bribe.

A poor thing that you

Came across

A battered thing

Among the rubble

A distant stadium

Whispered its crowds.

And the snake made of colours
Will welcome me into myself –
My all-attentive skin's
A page of hunger.

Make do with what I know
Pure want a closing down silence.
It leaves the clear high
Singing undisturbed,

Should maybe end
All in heap of fragments.
Today is a sense of walking
Out into empty street and sky

And I liked it, walking out
In blameless weather
As if all the things in the world were
Imagination's unfinished spectacle

I am. The human. Let me haunt you
Just here behind your shoulder
And I'll be seeing what comes towards us
Each vacant face awaiting occupation.

So will a loving claw relax
So, let it open
Mirror to which
I steer's blind light
Is somewhere else, you
Held me, there, and did not spill a drop.

I, a poor fire
Parents being the ones
To whom I never spoke
Refusing everything as I was bound
I must confess I
Feel the words crumble in my mouth.

Here alongside the park, a wolf
We each patrol our border
He is a mask, two small gold eyes
More elegant than any dog.
Contact with humans blunts them
Can't you see? His dead patrol.

That night I daresay all were blind
Till I became, the stranger
Until I walked out into air like this
Swarming breast. A city. Any one
Would do for walking in. I'd made
A complicated pact with silence.

Last night I dreamed about my father

Only he was a famous poet.

There is just me in the crowd

And a smell of japonica apples

Where I sit in October sunlight

Drinking my coffee in the park.

My name is

Appetite I sing

Greeting Want

Hollowed out by language
The fruit half-eaten
Where a band of light lay across the cloth.

In the chateau five blown ostrich eggs
On a table made of twenty two kinds of stone –
A house, whose answer came to nothing.

But the bird I glimpsed this morning
Large head for its body, long slender beak, exotic.
Its greeting flashed,

And the frog with a bright green back
Perched anxiously on the edge of a saucepan
When I came down to breakfast.

A flower out on the dune
Opened its yellow silk pavilion
Next to the fish thrown a hundred yards inland.

In the forest of lost content
A child who wonders
What kind of a perfume is flesh.

August, early morning, a chill
Leans in, some ripeness hangs, but
Not quite ready.

Abruptness of possession
Almond of flesh, and how we were
Stayed, last night, in front of a window of stars.

Behind the Roman altar underground
A patient green of moss
Grows in a saucer of light.

At the hill's foot
A gateway of eroded angels
Draws space down into its shelter.

Their substance simply fell into the air,
A bone of light, as if we
Put on all this flesh in answer.

The humming-bird hawk moth breakfasts beside us.
His hunger is exact
In front of a bush of promises.

My hunger is the space I fill.
Before devouring I describe my food
As if sawing at the branch where I sit.

Litter of crumbs, what's left unsaid
The painting stays, a piece of cloth
And always an exactness of enough.

Voided, what space
The language hollows out.
There is this lateness of becoming,

Here in the roadside pond
Carp rising to the surface
Ghosting the afternoon.

I inspect the close growing,
Language in scarcity,
This fruit, its waiting to be taken.

Careful pods seeds blacken in, like letters,
Are an armature, that's lifted up
On to a clear, late page of sky

Then some deliberate tread –
A snail waits in the world,
Its patience in being known;

There were five on the edge of the dunes.
They all clung to the same stalk
Just above the beach's brute light

Here at the edge of the land
Where almost the last of the world I found
Was gnawing at its own stalk.

The Eastern Boroughs

Art / Work

That's right, keep it moving.
We have seen the spring and not been impressed.

It is tedious
Buying food under the trees. When we have
Heaped up enough grain

We'll whisper the truth in banks
Scatter it on the water
His mouth is in the air –

We have taken him out of the city
Clutching credit cards. Our funeral
Rites are a matter of dignity,
Gold leaf on a watery grave.

Creature

The creature has learned
To make itself music
Plucking and sawing
Away at the guts of itself.
Muzzle scraping the ground
It has learned to play with its mouth
In a special kind of a way,
Half-starved at evening here in a
City will learn to grow quiet.

CHARTRES

Saw it just after the war – they'd taken out all the glass.
Looked rather good.
                    The Ambassador.

Encrusted language, high altar under snow
As if there were meaning without sign
A word made stone, and waking
It helps us to be dressed in light
Such as hesitates on stone –
Yes this might settle the hours.
Imagine the sky a roof of glass.
Language will get us outside it,
A labial softness pressed
Against the hardness of teeth.
It is the animal part of speech,
A fattening – then all at once
The doors swing open in the house of silence,
The window-shutters folded back
Like ears. I can imagine
Being emptied into all that music
Such as might sing
Free   the damaged
                    half of me.

Bungalow: 'La-Mer'

This shallow box is made of glass and wood
To have a word in front of it.

It is as if the word
Were prelude to some other music,

Perhaps the distant, lifting edge
Of water that you can't quite see from here.

But the sea is not a house, and this one
Having two birds in front of it

Which could be gulls or pigeons,
Stone or plaster, and are painted white

Frames the distance with its word.
Once inside and seated

All in that gleaming grave together
Would silence be the best of us?

Out walking early I had thought of them
In their low-windowed house

Being born each day into the sun
With each fresh waking, dewfall on a page

Until one day they'll slip away
And leave this name scorched on a piece of wood –

For the time being it simply lifts
Its puzzling hyphen.

Today we're headed for the shore, but this?
It brings us close but still it holds us off,

Feather of air, a dying breath
Confronting ocean fronted by a word.

Edge

The god has gone back under the waves
Uselessly uselessly trying to breathe his name –
Watch each one falter just before it breaks.
He left their irretrievable margin.
His were the eyes that saw the tilted land
Where a life was waiting for us.
It grows out of a sort of mist
And the new house built on the edge of the cliff,
With the traffic behind, is a palace of views,
An entire life lived inside inverted commas.
Walking up through a rain-soaked wood,
Its speckledy light effects, you reach the viewpoint.
You stand there waiting for the photograph,
Focussing on the too-much of it.
The water is an unusual sort of grey.
Someone made it look easy then disappeared
Who met with such a satisfying end,
But now the sun has come out,
And these are our defeats the sea is smiling with.

Out Walking, Again

In the City a stench of white hyacinths,
Monstrous-headed daffodils. A prison-shaped dream
Was the future, like a vista closing behind me
With a flourish. I'd resorted to vengeful watching.

Be seated now – the fat man
Sweats slightly eating his food as a punishment.
These diners, how squalid they look when seen from above
Perched above the ruins of a meal.

Shelves of whole cheeses are ranged in a window –
Their dense expectant silence,
The sum of these vestiges a vain crust of buildings.
There is so much inside an empty sculpted head

Where a man absents himself from himself
Even if it does taste of the open air.
In an empty landscape I remembered wanting,
Chatting with the sybil

But standing as close as this
They people the unpeopled air,
These knowing faces, then look up –
Sunlight's estrangement of the whole facade.

ORFEO

Saying neither No nor Yes
And always hurried on like this
He travels toward birdsong
Through the cool draughts of air
Blown down here in damp gusts,

Passing the roots of trees
That have a hold on silence
Imagining he's roused
The one who slept down there.
This time he'll bring her back.

He'd gone to ground like lightning, down after
Something imagined in the after-dark,
That fearful thing, to make it sing.
Should he turn round now, what will he see
Mirroring an absence?

Nevertheless like Grandmother's Footsteps
He senses a quick light tread of statues
Behind him breaking into movement,
Each foot planted in silence.
"Was what I tried to conjure there already?

Down here I am given
Desire to drown in, darkness to dream myself.
I carry my body of work,
Taking it forward. It fills
The space that's closing up behind me."

And so, remembering days
Of waking early to float downstairs,
Words gathering round him like a press of quills –
Flight is the only answer, mastered
By the change, so he might move

Upwards and into a slow arrest of air
To be all watching.
Claws shrivelled with excitement
He'll try to find the one swaying perch
In all that blandness.

But can the bird recover
Its track, before scattering
Into an insect-flight of words?
One's circling in that dreadful hollow
He's coming out from now, it spirals

Upward into the moment.
His open arms extend into the silence.
"Being here I don't know what to say"
So turns, to where she goes from him
And with that meaning marries half the sky.

It Was

in a painting. The way the light had
of falling just there
and, seeing how it was, you felt
it might start to make you happy.
Here are the three figures
who are turning towards each other,
in the drapery flow half-
seated and half-floating
and if they are all anchored
this is because of an arm
reaching out for and grasping
a jug. It is something quite personal,
a particular moment
but at the same time so
much out-there and not-you –
as if it is you are being reached
out, and about to touch
a concealed remoteness,
an otherness which becomes
you and so
by this oblique route
here I am being
found, at home in the world.

Missing Plinth

A litter of memorials –
Helicopter-like one hangs there
Shadowing an absence.
He'd crossed a city grown abruptly quiet.
The gallery was a dream-like warren of rooms
And only one painting, somewhere inside.
Perhaps it was the one
Where the half-bandaged god
Was taken into the ground
And if he yelled in the beginning
It surely must have been for lack of self.
Now, hanging in that final room,
He wondered, is it this
That outlasts being devoured, all
Painted surface and its paradox of depth?
Aching, he rose from sleep and it was like
Being born again into the air
Turning to look back, one final time,
At the building, its facade
Lifted into the day's first light
And calm as a missing statue's brow.

Exhibit

A terror of not being seen has flown to the walls.
The painting is what makes you notice an edge.
Its landscape froths greens and blues.
A divided self just stays
Splashing about in the colour shallows
As if it were walking around in an eye.
It makes an arch of colour
In Hoxton, a day in October two thousand and two
Whose conjunction of event – the sun,
Turning of the earth and cloud
Being moved by wind – have all combined
To make this patch of sunlight, coming in
From outside, slowly move
Over a landscape's painted silence.
For once I am thoroughly here
Where a piece of blue is the name of the sky.
Arriving in unlit corners of the self
It tried to make the world come real –
But 'I' is this epiphany of absence.
It stepped back when that moment
Called consciousness of self
Split me away. Still falling
I'll settle on the room's four final walls.

LANYON AT ST IVES

There was this man, passionate about gliding, who fell out of the sky's silence and into the landscape he'd painted all his life – first a cracked vertebra, then a blood clot that tricked the brain and that was how he died. 'But I have always relied on some basic feeling of infinity', he wrote.

I look out over the deserted
January beach,
Watch the advancing crash
Of waves in brilliant sunshine.
Behind me are his paintings,
A line of them on their curve of wall.
There is the way this enormous curve of glass
Silences the sea out there.
Between it and the canvas
Is where for now I am,
The sea-theatre framed and a life
That stops at the frame.
I'd imagined that what I chose out there –
The pebble, the wave-worn wood –
Had chosen me. Not wasting a moment of being
I'll breathe on the glass, to watch
The breath I am condensing there
While sea crawls up the beach
And it takes all afternoon.

He is somewhere here, at an angle to landscape
Under its final coating of sunlight.
Today such winter sun's a strength of shadow.
Moving aside to let the light pass
Where I go out into a fading afternoon
I pass closed galleries, out-of-season,
Walk through a gloom of municipal gardens
Still looking for him, the man who fell from the sky.

In the sculpture garden winter palm-tree's rattle –
I turn round, hearing the flap of wings,
Dove perched on the self-monument.

Authored

Getting towards the end it is
The silences he hears grow round him
And something that comes knocking at the door –
It is that selfsame sense of lack
Gets closer with the insistence of rhyme.

Struggling back to where his past began
He'd tried to write himself into the story.
'I was the chosen one
In my coat of imaginary colours.'
Could it exist without the writing down?

He had found a way of not being near,
A mind looking after itself
Like the bird that whiles away time in the air.
'At this distance one can be serious',
Sending the words out there

But now it seems to come from further off
Like an echo in retreat,
A shout going distant in the afternoon.
As if dawdling on one foot art
Gave him the illusion of being.

'I' folded into 'you' and trying to find
A way to it, as the split tree's lightning self
Once held to that crack in the light,
It is as if he is filling the wound with sound.
There is something eaten day by day

In a perfect solitude resists
These steady encroachments of silence.
Now like a *kouros* there's something
Steps forward, one quiet foot leading
Out of the gathering emptiness: 'I am

What hovered by your shoulder
Attending to the page you held.
I'm moving round in front of you.
It's almost at an end
And you are my last hope of silence now.'

The Feelings

You will know when it finally leaves you
Disappearing as if it folds up inside
Itself, turns into a sign.
Love made this thing.
Anger is also its name

And he remembered them out of his childhood
Or rather, as if they were
What he remembered remembering
He thought, the feelings were like
Animals – part familiar and part strange.

But still there was this
Miracle of the sign he'd found,
Substanceless yet inexplicably solid
And it could replace
So much of the world.

The Good Things

The good things were
In there   but breath
It was cold on the pane
When he reached out writing his name there

One of the first
Winters it was of being sent away
And what he wrote, it was one more
Sign of an absence

But as if there were
A ripening   of the not-quite-visible
Or was it just the
Translation of an echo,

His life? He felt it was like
A novel of which he had never
Read more than the first few pages,
Such fullness of expectation

Being caught in the morning sunlight
And he could never quite bear to read more.
It is still there,
A book that waits all night beside its owner.

The good things, like
Berries in a frozen winter landscape,
Sun-flare on ice puddles –
It became a picture ah those feelings.
He'll watch and watch

While 'now' is a photograph flooded with early light,
A pavement café, Atget, Paris 1930.

It is empty of people. Why is he drawn each
Day to this absence, sunlight on stone?
'I wrote the words on the way to somewhere.'
A child's hand reaching
Out and not quite finding

Imagined the glass cold as time
Laid over it –
Nostalgia was a name for it.

The book of 'he' – this
Particle, might come to know itself
Out in the quiet rain.

The good things, he saw them.
They were in the exhibition.

These were desires
Gone to the walls,
There to take refuge in their frames.

Here was Christ in the garden,
Day breaking already
And he is back fresh from the earth
Painted in earth colours – 'Noli me tangere'.
He shrinks away
From the woman in the red skirt
Who is down on her knees and reaching forward.
Here is another,
His mouth a perfect O

As if the man in the painting
Were condemned like this to sing forever

And leave us to wonder
What we should do, out here, with his remains of sound.

The setting being 'The Artist's Room:
Rue du Cherche-midi' –
Bedstead, window and a small table.
But there are afternoons to nowhere,
Mute pressure on the page
That scarcely harms the paper,
The frame being home to someone
In the street of searching afternoon.

And later, seeing himself
Far out at sea – this was
Turner's 'Sea Monsters at Sunrise',
Light bundled up in the paint,
And where the light fell
On the picture, to join it
He was
So mysteriously *there*,
The watching-self as epilogue

Walking on through the exhibition
And their faces all looked
Out at him through the art.

Deaf

The London Plane . . . believed to be of hybrid origin, a cross between the American and the Oriental Plane, or chenar . . . so prized was the shade of this tree that, when they transplanted it to France, the Romans extracted a 'solarium' by way of a tribute from any of the natives who should presume to put his head in its shade.

Isaac de Souza
From Goa, wearing a deaf-aid
Is on 'permanent supply',

Would rather teach English,
Is still waiting to hear – perhaps
The Council's Disability Quota?

Or, paradoxically,
Will Equal Opportunities floor him
Since the job's not been properly advertised?
(There's no money to advertise it).

He can always unhook
The piece of plastic –
So deafness may have its uses.

Meanwhile I am picking over
The bones of this city
In one of its bleaker eastern suburbs.
The traffic is, well, traffic,
The maimed saplings we pass
A lesson to us all.

"I mean, I've been learning
This language for most of my life"
As he waits downstairs in the staffroom
For his timetable, in the school
Where I am teaching English,
Both connoisseurs of
Impossible grammars
In the the plane-tree's, the chenar's shade.

Language Lesson

Refugee trying to fasten
A red rose to the windscreen.

Grown in a greenhouse
It's not quite the colour of blood.

Enormous hidden populations,
City afloat on some sort of raft

But safe in here in here we're doing the language dance,
It's English as a Second Language

And that means I am in here
Teaching the words to do their best to find you.

When the time comes
To fix these words in your mouth

There is that space between us
And the language is like the news

Just before it reaches you.
It waits in the air, weighs down your bag.

This evening, walking down
A street whose rubbish blows towards us

Why should it resemble
The wasted landscape of a dream?

'In Turkey' you had told me
'History is difficult.

We have to learn the Sultans
Whose names all sound the same'.

You talked about Hikmet and you showed me
A greyish photograph – your father,

Some sort of Party gathering years ago
Somewhere near a lake and I had thought

The most of politics might be
An intelligent refusal

Watching your tower block subside
Into an effusive sunset.

At the Centre

A usual kind of paralysis
Installed here – is it compassion fatigue?
The years one spent in there,
Its administrative clatter,

The years of lost good causes.
Another meeting has been called
Sings the party of permanent government.
What meeting in a meeting?

These are the Minutes, read them, be unshriven
And how the live thing in you suffers
Open at its most tender part.
Maybe it's an illness I've subscribed to.

I came out, then I went back in,
Years spent climbing an endless staircase
Like an aural illusion, a note in music
That going up and up gets nowhere.

For half an hour or so perhaps I'll come
Closer to the one wish in your head.
We've each a code embedded into plastic.
The machine grows hot, all afternoon.

Post-modern are
Greek columns waxing lyrical in sunlight
Beside a half-emptied river,
Bitter the polluted air that eats them.

Which architect designed this mania,
Arranging pronouns in the social order?
Being privatised will hide behind a logo
Even unto the air we breathe,

Passing abandoned dockyards,
Extending to the city's river delta.
And here's the one who always wore
His wound on the outside,

A suit of lights. He said
'This is the nothing I was meant to bring you'
But here consumer particles
Move all too quickly to be counted.

In a tower block beside a river
Just touched by morning sunlight
I imagine him learning the names
Scrawled on the walls there,

And, hot on the track of exile,
Is a voice weaving its way
Like the ghost of a refusal
Reflected in passing shop windows.

So we go on defined by our absences.
This is the shop windows' message,
The carefully chosen colours
That flare with a dry radiance.

Shortage, depletion,
Headlines manufacturing scarcity:
'You are what you shall not have'
But do you remember –

It was gold falling out of the sky,
Those trees blurred in a hot heavy wind
Engendered by the thrashing blades
To what purpose? And then, this intoxication,

It crept along at ground level
In a haze of scented smoke, and the men
Who pass and who will not be recognised
Are the dream we endure, of the parcel recovered.

Dig

The thing was to induce the vision of Portland Place to generalise itself. This is precisely the fashion however after which the prodigious city as I have called it does on occasion meet halfway those forms of intelligence of it that it recognises. All of which means that at a given moment the great Philistine vista would itself perform a miracle, would become interesting for a splendid atmospheric hour, as only London knows how, and that our business would be to understand it.
     Henry James

Sir Leonard Woolley, archaeologist and excavator of Ur was born in a house on this site.
     Plaque on a railway bridge in Hackney, East London.

1
Just opposite MC Breakers, Crash Repairs
As if the plaque announces someone waiting

To excavate silence, golden harp
Where birdsong tends a small wilderness.

But walking here, you might well ask
Where have they moved it to?

Here it's that inner-city mix
Of quasi-pastoral and light industrial,

A haze of leafage over blackish water
And the running children with their bright names.

Lives sifting down here are lived
At such a distance from the appalling centre

Where imagination falters
As figures jump over a screen –

Cuneiform flash, Sunday silence
In the City, it's another idea

That hides behind darkened window-glass.
It only reflects the briefest of passing selves.

The guard inside's half-sunk in shadow –
Enormous silence of a uniform.

2
Walking away from the grave-plot of self
And all the voices in my head

I am limping into the future again.
Sundays like this are where the district wakes

As if greeting its own silences,
Ragwort, anchusa rising up through pavements,

June's squadrons of derelict roses,
Its pigeons doves that make the most of it.

It was something the light fell into
On afternoons of sun-shadowed

Architecture, when buildings take
Their bite out of time and in its museums

The perfect stillness of so much life
You cannot reach to through the brutal glass.

Outside again, the hurrying, suited
Figures cut out of the dark part of sunlight

Seem one-dimensional mostly,
Disappear as if into a photograph.

Or else apocalyptic
January sunshine, Camden Town

Lets say, in Royal College Street
Rimbaud's out walking with Verlaine.

There's architecture's suspension of time,
Oddness of these extraordinary terraces

As if once abandoned but now occupied
By a race of punctilious, anxious barbarians.

Here was archaic ground, sweat smell of grass,
Still rising from one mown and final field.

'One good fuck deserves another'
Said its goddess, afterwards

Lying back in those sublime muds,
Baked earth for building, writing

And they were coming in from the fields
Looking for money, filling the burial grounds.

3
I saw it once, the almost-promised city,
Wan streetlamps, idylls of rust.

This city, not a place exactly –
It was more a thing I'd balanced in my mind,

Crossed and recrossed by the absolute
Purity of bird flight.

I'd haunted its edge everywhere,
Discovered, I thought, the last indigene.

As if tricked into coming alive
And tracked to his favourite watering-hole

He was some words scrawled on a wall
Where language came to collide with the world

And had there been still more words
I'm sure I might have found them

Like something abruptly come upon
In an empty square, clatter of pigeons' wings.

But as it was I simply went on walking,
Being filled with something that I could not name.

Shores

The nightmare-withering,
   Something used up, then voided
In structures of rage.

You. Mouth
   Crying, in sand ex-
tinction. The beautiful structures

That came to anchor limit,
   Far dome a
Presence in the mind.

So early in the
   Text it is
Light walks.

What reflection implies: this
   Stillness, the not-
Broken all-mothering gaze.

Being born it was required
   I think myself somewhat
Further into that glass –

Matter as the
   Reflection of nothing,
And moments to come, of such

Absolute strangeness
   As I am being taken out into the air.
The reflection stays.

How it was to be alive –
   A statue hesitating in a dream?
In your 'iris dream' you saw

This wonderful new flower.
   You put it in your mouth.
How could the whole thing fit, you wondered.

More other than stone or leaf
   Your face is between my hands.
Outside day climbs from nothing

And, like an afterthought, behind us
   This huge, shallow pool has spread
An entire carpet of reflections.

Will this other remember?
   It turns to us its face of absence.
Branches stiffen in the wind.

Ours is the regular procession
   Each day like pilgrims
Through pine trees to a barren shore.

I remember how we once came
   Shorewards – and now a single sheet
Of water will suffice

To erase the
   Commerce we have
Had with this edge.

Tongue's brave in its salt armour,
   Full day on all our skins,
The names of water drying.

There is a sea-squirt
  Eats its brain
Having no further use for it.

Now here is a thing that I keep finding,
  Dried up fish thrown way inland.
It is like an emptied purse.

Here by this root I'll creep,
  My flesh a thing apart,
Pale branched standard

Naked-awkward and nowhere belonging.
  I'd carried an ache
Once buried in her careful weight

Until, not knowing when or how
  It was I would be fed
The world was brought to my lips

And appetite was found.
  Now sight I am now breath have come
Into the bay of her eyes.

Going right in,
  This stranger-cup
Warm boundary, becoming name.

Describing, world as
  Consolation
I am the oddness, flaw in the glass.

Plucked from the tree of names
  Are plants emerging from our patch of gravel,
Each raising its leaf, its flower.

Space being a 'perfect black body'
   There is heat-exchange all night long
Out at the end of the atmosphere

Where language takes me
   To an edge of nothing.
So on a night of perfect stillness

Air charged with water cools until,
   The dew-point reached, the table face
And chairs are pimpled with the drops,

This mirroring of nothing
   As intimate as a wet seat.
Next night we'll lean the chairs

Against the house
   To catch its stored-up heat
So that the seats stay dry.

I'll begin to invent the sea again.
   Single page is lonely knowledge.
Just caught by the departing wave

An edge of nothing
   Is taken back, into the planet's
Deep inward curve of matter.

I think I am as near
   As I shall ever be.
Each wave must surely heave itself

Into one final moment,
  A deckled edge and then
Our perfect page-like stillness.

I had a page, that listened
  To a movement of the wind,
All that blueness held

So easy in the embrasure of a window.
  I was with you in the emptiness.
Your stranger-nearness, now

This veil might lift
  Its cloud of signifiers. In there
A child's still swarming over

A breast. As if the food
  Being lifted to each mouth
Were to cry out its name.

                Soustons, Southwest France

At the Victoria and Albert Museum
What can it mean, like this to
  Label a man Ocean?
This bloated head

Being fixed to a fountain floor,
  His office underneath these waters –
All its chairs are standing round

Never to be occupied.
  In such peculiar light
The wooden panels lift and stir.

Eventually I struggled out
   Past the quiet attendant
Into the bone-white light outside –

Poseidon still at my back
   What slow ascent, staircase of frozen waves,
Preposterous clerk to those waters.

Family

Whatever was it, the meaning
Of all that closeness, being at home together?
It's as if we were not sure
Quite what to do with it,
There was so much that went without saying
And I still find it hard to explain
The silences, surrounding us
Like pools of dusty light.
Today I found the pottery bowl,
The one I gave my father, a Christmas present,
When I was thirteen or so
As if it were my silence I was giving him
Inscribed with its puzzle of pattern.
I turn it round and round,
This object that is all
An openness and a containing
Watching the pattern shift and grow
And I remember the care
With which I went out by myself
And chose it, almost fifty years ago
On a fine December morning.

Fathering

At the Old Windmill, Gazely, Norfolk

A body – now it gives me
A particular strong earthy silence
And elements of sunrise

His frame being settled deep,
His portrait staring back
From seventy years ago

As if the light being
Glimpsed for the first time
The chemicals all bloomed.

Some inexplicable hope
Settled back onto that shiny surface.
No longer able to make speech

His smile still has an unused look.
It was as if he'd found
A way to put off living

And that was how death found him.
It used him quite suddenly,
A coin fresh-minted under ground.

Reflection   like a shoulder
In water, it heaves
Upward to a stilled surface.

It is someone there
Wanted the water deep
But now, a coming into breath,

Shoulder smeared with earth
Being stained with an agreement of sunrise –
He turned away to the sky.

The stars have broken out
Into their brutal glitter.
Frost-roughened trees

Lead up to a brick tower.
In there my children are asleep
Stacked one above the other.

In its doubt, its
Wakefulness seed stirs.
The year turns on its black heel.

As if it were being written
In the sleeping child
(Can I sleep honestly?),

These fathers, battered
Antique medals'
Faint impress in the plush.

Years taller now,
The poem. Lies and whispers.
So it lasts, another lifetime.

Sperm-blink. The flesh is all I took
Away from such an act,

Little worm of light
Issuing across the border,

Secret serpent —
Have you the knack?

A line of light   you
Serpent-crept beneath a door.

Now child stand up,
I in my coat of many colours.

In light-array the
Want-serpent is battle-worn

An open door the light-barrier
That once put me to flight.

Pheasant croak, faint
Roar of a two mile
Distant road.

These fathers I have found
Are what is this way coming,
Their breath-filled lightness is

A remoteness of being
Walking out over
Frozen December fields.

And now there are these five
Women, and one gaudy priest
Who calls himself a father —

A word made flesh
Has found its way to this
Raised heap of flint and brilliant glass.

Swelling in its window is
An easy blur of light.
It pauses, here on the floor

And how much of my childhood
Like this was stayed, withdrawn
Into such held-back watching.

In a dream I once made such a house,
Stone thing, container I contained
To grow inside, to look out over

The new fields growing
Grey with daybreak,
A self of buried rivers.

Yes, today I should wear myself like a leaf.

Early in my silence
At daybreak, scored by the sound

Of an aeroplane passing the world
The voice I am still tells it in my ear –

How a loving nature
Was frightened out of itself.

I go back to a heap of meaning.
My home has been such words

To construct an aching mirror
And take this tongue to hell.

But all that time an untouched thing
Was elsewhere looking after itself

And now the scar remembers
An ordinary hurt

Being what I have to show.
I'll weight it now towards you

And the scar fades to a tune.

Orchard: Upper Pant Farm, Gwent

What's bitten into is so cold
The flavour feels like something
Condensed out of October air.

Walking in your orchard –
Red Bramleys. Bending
To take them from the soaking grass,

Fruit of a fallen world.
A coming into breath is
Hearing the silence where I am

And the life of each leaf –
How it hangs still, before the fall.
It is something painfully clear.

Out here each fruit's a ripened brow
At daybreak, chilled with dew.
Our still-lives, being a meal withheld,

Are brought to table.
Each fruit is this
Perfected silence.

Self-portrait: Rembrandt at Kenwood

I walked across the Heath, and came
To this off-white dead house
One year later on a sunlit morning.

Finding the self-portrait, I
Being held by it, the look
Back at me's an indrawn breath

And the sun is at the window
Hiding the pigment with its radiance, where
Reflections jostle in its glass

So now it is my portrait, looking back
And full of all the unsaid things.
I am silent now,

A distant substance, fallen on by light.
The personal is so remote,
It is something found

The other side of all this hindering brightness,
A stranger-self that I might
Come upon, behind the years of

Pecking at the dome
Greeting myself at each return,
Each solitary epiphany.

It takes a life to shore it up.
No sooner reached it is abandoned
And then the sky dazzles, threshold of breath,

My hand on a doorknob of air.
Here I'm encountered, in hints and whispers.
This is the strangeness of the building

And what could I bring except my silent
Shield of recognition?
The face still watches in the dead house

For each lonely visitant.
The portrait's like a mask put on
Called 'consciousness of self'. Outside

I'll find myself in the rush of light,
The play of it on stone, on water
Until, it seems, I am:

Such radiant fortress.

After / Word, The Apology

The day: it draws me up at five,
First serious light
And I am trying not to put

That pious exhalation
Round an 'I', that
Thing like a faint nimbus.

These volumes all
Are only what I
Might have simply said

To each of you, there being
Simply the two of us.
It is our ordinary fame,

Still has an odd innocence –
Each time happened on it might
Be fresh and startling news.

It is a fallen world,
Blooms and moulds.
Mouth stuffed with petals

I exist the writing machine –
I am starting to dislike it,
This voice that comes off the page

And have walked
Through days of silence
Meaning to amend it.

A Place Like Here

'I want to set off for the place where I am.'
                    D.H.Lawrence

In Cornwall

Early morning up the dew-wet track following the blaze of sun,
Each sensation separate and early.
Look back again at tended iron-age fields.
A yacht sleeps on the stretched ocean.

By midday, stare out of the circle, nothing but grass.
Sea wind and sun will polish you like a mirror.
The church at Morvah, in an elbow of road,
Hayfields, the doze of sea:
Distant smells of animals and men.

Late afternoons of strong sunlight, dogs statuesque in the road.
A rooftop stained with lichen.
The midday page and the midnight page.

On Arran

This morning there is something
That drives me from my bed
To inhabit the shoreline quiet.
Earth's cover wastes.
Birds pick at it
Where it curls like a damp page.
There are pipits, insects,
And one seal's soapstone head
That's caught in a patch of sunlight.

Young guillemot, front
Smudged with oil –

It looked at first
As if it were nesting
In a tuft of grass
Till I got closer.
An eye black as oil
Flush with the head,
A neck that turns through
One hundred and eighty degrees.
Woven into the system
I am as quiet as the bird is
As the tide slaps closer, closer.

Over from Kintyre
Clouds rush to fill the morning.
Moving further across
The boulders, I am an awkward
Body now older
But on it a quick eye, to
Hook me here like a seed
As I move over this
Raised beach – for us, is it,
This stone and water garden?
I turn round to confront
Waves marching, in their pale of air
While from the red
Sandstone cliff there comes down
A curtain of blown water.
Finding a piece of wood
Dried feather-light as paper
I find I like this margin
Where the sea beds down in the grass.
This beach of boulders
Is pinkish, pale ochre, grey.
Plants colonise it
Existing here at the margin

Quite without visible means.
Silverweed has red threads
Extending among the stones.
There's orache, sowthistle,
Sandwort, wild beet,
Clumps of daisies
Above the cast-up lines of seaweed –
There's a line of green
A line of brown
A line of orange, and then
A stone wall I shall watch for ages.

Duddon Valley

On a day like this the furthest hills are blue
   Seem near. A friendly sucker
Waves in its warm pool of air.

Bracken races off up turning silver.
   The failure of description to supply the want,
To flesh it out and give it substance.

We seek confirmation among the boulders
   To anchor ourselves to their remote substance,
Pile cairns to mark the footpath story.

Everywhere information is verified.
   We look up the plants in the book,
The little red-haired sundew, the pure stonecrop –

Beside them garden flowers look blunted.
   There's the murmur of water.
Up on the mountain now and it's almost noon

The sea, being twelve miles off
   Is a bar of blue.
Over it stands one cloud.

I imagine the life down there, cars
   Changing gear, a morning leaning
Forward into its press of traffic

And all at once, being here I'm there
   Being caught at the head of the beach
In that rush of wind and sunlight.

Isle of Purbeck

Who has made the discovery of all this
On a day risen again without blemish.

I mean, today's
Stone-pale spring light

As if the quarry'd
Invaded the town.

"I have made up the single bed for you."
The landlady's brain-damaged daughter
Moans behind her door.
She is named after a flower
And the orange bedspread and curtains
Are a story everyone else has forgotten.

Chapman's pool   a still morning.
Empty bay behind me.
Here are such soft cliffs.
By these fossil-rich shales imagine

Landfall, across eye of water.
                              Today
The blackthorn is in full flower,
Makes a white track onto a crowded island.
Now I am walking between
This shelf of land and a nothing of sunlight
Reflected in water two hundred feet below.
Standing in front of the sea
I can hear the birds sing behind me
From a land of faded notices.
I watch how the small sail blends with the wind,
The faint stir far below
Of water over a pattern of seaweed.

Strolling at midnight
Below swelling balconies
Hearing the slop slop slop on the seawall.
Next day the brown heath
Trembled in a lens
Of heat, sails
Bellied round the point.

And reached an abandoned quarry
Like a temple set into the cliff.
I sprawled among fallen stone there
Then came around the point
To the Great Globe in the afternoon,
Where, on its shelf of garden,
Its absurd facts erode.

That voice   the place
Where *he* blends into *I*,
Pronominal interface,
The sky as border.

Shrubs leaned out over this
Stretch of late-glittering water.
The tea-room was in a sort of Folly.
I went on down through a wood,
White Narcissus, faint-scented,
And as far as the beach.
In front of the bay's shallow curve
Crabs and lobsters were trapped
In a brick pool down on the Front.
They scuttled to the edge as if to shelter.
Mind and body both slowed leaning over
To watch, in the daze of late afternoon –
Such beautiful machines!

I stayed and stayed
Being so much here the tenant,
At last, of my own silence.

Isle of Purbeck, Dorset

On Sark

Anger   paranoia   aggression towards A   feeling of central 'blackness'.

A description of the room, description of the elements

The fridge
breathes gently
Cockcrow at 4AM

My dreams leak out and into a fellow sunrise, the rose transfer. The awful nightmare of laying everything waste in one outburst of savage violence. 'I' manoeuvres 'you' into impossible positions then strikes.

Gulls resting in the fields.
cockcrow to cockcrow, echoes
fuschias in tides
the sea in its rock temples,
a 'well-made poem'
children of drought – the work conceived in fear
a dark red up in the roof of the cave
sounds of voices, strung out across the road

deep in the well the eye of water
the 'I' of water
       and thou   a sea-grey day
the sea extends its influence over fields

All this sea-gazing, why? Desire for annihilation while sitting on a bench, 'In Memory . . .' My ILEA / gun dream, then anxiety lurking in the curtains. The man I met talking about rain – the way he kept hitting his fist against his palm. 2 middle-aged ladies, typical Sark holidaymakers.

The bay sinister and then cosy houses – all in miniature. Voices soft and insistent between the hedgerows. Innocent delight. Quarrelling in the rain. And for the first time that autumnal smell of the leaves after rain.

A's watercolours, postcards, my photos – and a few drawings I did as well? A large slow horse appears and disappears at a crossroads. No cars of course but the occasional tractor. Recapturing innocence, as in certain forms of hunting (birdwatching, photography). Here. Greys and silvers on the sea, an evening of uncertain cloud, a single very faint gleam of sun.

Time is a room just near
seizing the day
but things become more *observed*, less a shaft going straight through
                                                                             one.

Out at 9am, very quiet, a dazzle of sun on the sea over to the left and breeze like flickering eyelashes on the hedgerow and on the distant water. Sea very blue now over the tops of the hedges. Mill, church tower, and the Pilcher Monument, small but just visible, holding the skyline together. The Methodist cemetery, grass close-cropped, very plain stones worn and covered in lichen and mostly quite unreadable. Arranged in odd groups on the brown shoulder of turf, and in the distance a fragment of sea like a butterfly's wing. Thinking of the traditional folk dance we saw last time, the old men and women dressed up, moving slowly, the moves of the dance so often repeated – but why did it look like a rehearsal for something else?

The old silver mines, small chimneys rising above the bracken and here and there the spoil tips, whitish heaps still uncovered by any vegetation. Imagining silver bled out of the rock. Port a la Jument's in shadow but the kestrel hovering above us is in the sun, the sunlight showing through a speckled curtain of feathers. A solitary tern hitting the water then swerving back up a silvery fish held sideways in its beak. A raven being harried by a group of magpies above the bay. Cormorant, just its neck and bright yellow beak visible above the waves. A whole flock of them, around sixty, appeared round the headland and headed out over the sea. Where they settled on the water I could just make them out with the binoculars. Late sunlight in Dixcart wood, insects making a really loud humming, then suddenly all visible in the dusky light, suspended at different levels.

Just for a moment the words have a bloom on them, it could so easily fade

His phrase 'the bliss of ordinariness', is us in our lives

Ivy swarming with red admirals.

The occasional butterfly right down on the beach.

Watching myself approach
The island: shavings of distance.

Beside a sunlit sea's
My depleted parentage –

It is what the sea has drowned
With its alphabet
          A ruined game

And here I am, perfect, with a stone to sit on.
Like a lens clearing
The memory
Airs itself, sailing away
Will see me, where I dwindle
To a blade of grass.

Next day, the Islander –
Its going-away affairs droned overhead,
Archaic silver sky-stance.

Down here, the pleasures of free-wheeling!
Passing the pale hydrangea flares
Where fields verge into brightness.
What drifts across is dust or mist.
Beside the silver mines
We searched the whitish heaps of spoil.
A trace of habitation searched for –

A gate marked Private
Across a grassy lane. This watchful absence
Is what I shall become.
There are the others.
Now they squeeze past –
I'll let them go back the way they came.

Buff roads and high dust-whitened hedges
Hide conversations.
Barnacle galaxies on a face of rock.
Gull resting in a field.
The humble victories of sleep;
Cockcrow answering cockcrow.
The black snout of a fish
From under its lip of stone.

Anxiety, in a curtain, it hangs
There deprived.
The roof of the cave dark red, ferns growing up there,
Its mouth twice daily blocked by sea.
From the well the I of water, looks back up at me
A sea-grey day, its influence over fields.
Inland will equal
A pail of water dipped in sunlight.

He and She, on the beach at Grande Greve,
Two stones soak up the last of the sunlight.
The relief of turning back, up to land, its
Leaf-quiet and habitation.

Sitting on a bench inscribed In Memory:
I stare out over water
Is there a reward for all this watching?

Abraded stones stirred
Comfortably, down on the beach

While somebody's transistor
Was wearing away the morning.

Mist blurs, impelled
By a righteous sun to brightness

Suffused with
Birdsong in rainsoaked fir trees

And a smell of the sea again,
The damp earth full of signals.

Your paints blend and run with water.
Stones get worn to a planetary roundness.

They lie like offerings. The tide
Swells up to a listening beach.

I imagined the books in a future
Distance, printing like the fern's shadow,
Ink all a darkness of flight
On a page that is whitened with sunlight. This was
In a house my presence neared,

Yet overgrown, empty,
A place of becoming and ending. My ears
Are stopped with wax against that perpetual silence.

So what remains, of all that distance?
Vivid scripture of its blue.

You come home from the island jeweller's
With an agate in a ring – dark stone

Infused with white, this
Cloud-like drift, its permanence

Where a shack door empties the wind
Noon practises its palmistry
On wavering shadows.

Houses set back from the cliff
Are full-face to afternoon sunlight.
The local star exhausts its strength.

Out on the headland
Gorse-pods crackle open in the heat.
Sea has a mirror's distance, nearness.
A hawk escapes my eyes' cover.
Over and over
He searches still –
A useless treasure.

My being that took
'You' for a name
Was your white body a thorn invaded
And shelters in water,
Reflections massed at the point of meeting,
Dawdles on a bicycle:
It sees over hedges
The distance home

Swaying down to the
'Westerly dipping
Biotite-gneiss',

An angry work
Whose outcrops have cooled:
I pass Beau Regard's green shutters

Travel toward the sea.
Telephone wires soar and dip.
The water pours off its shelf.

I watch the birds on the wind.
Late afternoon, I come on my family
Like strangers out on the cliff.

We are dazzled standing beside
This memorial to the drowned sailors
In a feast of windy sunlight.

Channel Islands

Estuary

The marriage of biographies,
Yours and mine. Our obstinate
Freedoms light up the hedges.
Insect-shimmer in low-lying fields
While back in a house of stone pages are turning
A volume of our smiles.
There are disused factories overgrown with grass,
A spoor of production up split concrete lanes.

A peculiar darkish light
That prevails – a yellow field to our left
Where the flowers ride
And our intercourse, your body still fairer,

Abruptly the sky
And then the estuary, its gathered pools

In favoured silence
Approaching their horizon.

The estuary, no
Footpath through its solitary wet.
The water turns and heads in now

Joining itself, in swirls of conversation
Invades a mud bed with its prussian blue.
Crisp waves are filled with light –
It was a divine bed wind felt along
Where sea ran parallel to our voices.

The tide comes in at walking pace
A widening tongue of water
Bringing small fish, they don't
Swim so much as are carried
Along, drifting sideways, twitching.

The beach makes a crackling sound.
Bubbles rise in a froth.
Gulls are dots out on the level sea.

In rockpools the seaweed
Frond upon frond rises straight up
Steaming in the sun.

The sea licks the land
And the sands dazzle.

Turning landward the saltings
Are mounds of close grass
Threaded with channels.

Into this particoloured
Field of creation
We two moved
With caution,

Turned walked back
Into a bank of birdsong

Standing out some way in front
Of where the land fell away steeply
Blueish in haze.

In the egg, clearness –
It holds a dark speck.
The albumen clouds
To ripen in noisy woods.

Behind the dunes water captures
The bivalves, their opening tune.

Back in the town exploding on asphalt
Came a smell of the first fat raindrops.

For a long time
We went down lanes of conversation.
A factory glimmered in the haze.
The tide withdrew.
It left our voices chaired by wind
Which the sea takes up
Reflective in its air.

On the other side of the hill
I guess lips formed deftly for speech.
What I write is the distance,
'Dead ground' between here and the estuary –

Derelict farms,
Cemetery, waste-tip.
A train trundles across
Half-finished sentence I'm still gazing after,

Windless distance,
Points, on a line
Bursting with fractions,
A wafer of land
That's not sure where to go.

But just before you get there
You can smell water –

Going down there I'll take a look.

Or else the people
Whose ways are that bit foreign –

This factory, that
Fraying edge of cloud.
Likewise my torn verse,
Its blessing of disguise.
Enough to eat, but
Harder to read the ideas
Pierced by a flight of objects
Falling in a slow curve.

The town curdles
In a wide valley.
Shapeless in the cold
Lined faces
'Just like in Russia'.
DO IT ALL DIY

Suspended in the mirror
The driver's face looks small,
Chats up two girls as they get off.

We all hang over the valley
Its precipitous heaps of slag –

Surplus and spoil, waste ground,
Exchange of courtesies,
Houses along every ridge,
Bluffs of cold, worn outcrops
Where we have been and haven't.

MFI TESCO
Freshly turned banks of earth,
'Consumer durables' – imagine
One lit from all sides,
Lets say below that
Conifer-dark hill
And approached over long brown grass
To where it's resting just above the ground,
A meeting point of all these forces
It is both more and less than substance,
Hologram in a ruined valley.
Slowly the light of afternoon
Will spread and fill again.
The bus doors open with a sigh.

Back there the estuary's
Vague grass that rare birds fly among,
Remembering the factory –
A plundered temple
It floated in haze.

Llwnhendy / Swansea

The Lure

The river speaks an absence clearly.
I could not imitate
The accent if I tried

Calls across
To the Ferry –
Warkworth Hermitage,

Its rock, and the
Boat's faint clatter.

Bird-call, from the dark
Late summer trees,
A stillness over water.

   This riven homage
Among the rock's dim thunder.

Shell of what I am saying, these
  Boats are bobbing –
    One seen now from way above, it
Drifts, without a companion.

Now I am stilled to an acquiescence:
A midday glare's on things.
Kingfisher   tropical blue
Over the black water.

He flew quite straight –
How his motion is
And not one bit like mine

Where waterlights are polishing the grey trunks.
Return to the river's mud-coloured sublime,
Its faintly dimpled cheek,
River all in shade.
The angler is wrapped in its calms, brings
A cloud of insects like dust in flight.
He came clambering over the stained
Boulders, in his suit of olive green,
Rod so fine and whippy, attenuate phallus,
The string bag his keep-net vagina.
Athletic sea-trout – watch it leaping
From this so calm surface, fracturing sunlight.
Does he know how the
Sexual lure spreads on the water?

Others watch birds, their faces screwed up
In an agony of looking, for that remote thing,
Fledged dinosaur, ominous: the elusive rarity,
Hung round with notebooks, maps and binoculars
Watching or reaching down, what will
Burst from the sky- or water-blankness?

What the sea burns off
In early rays,
Residuum of mist,
 Is like an explanation
That I did not try.
A valley fills with cars.

We'll drive out to the hills.
I'll read my future in a pool of liquor –
Black Forest Gateau
At the Tankerville Arms.

Between the open-cast mine and the castle
Is a suburb of Thirties semis, discreetly set
Away from the old town and ours has
Walls hung with heavy papers, embossed
With an inscrutable pattern, extraordinary bright carpets,
Bowls, jugs, ashtrays and vases, surfeit of
Devices for holding things, every one empty.
A sort of winged easy chair, solid to the eye
Topples when you touch it, as do the porcelain
Taiwan ladies. Just across the field
Is the castle whose keep has
Locked rooms preserved for a local duke.
Everything will be preserved if not sanctified.

There will be a pageant, hence locals
In their motley streaming over
The cricket field at twilight –
Look, here's another one coming
In dressing gown and sandals.

So, to skirt all this,
At a watching distance
I look down, again at that slow water.
"The traveller, returning in the evening"

And I did not cross the river.
The ferryman – I only saw him once,
'English Heritage: No Private Boats To Land',
This being an island of notices.
Crossing the playing fields so I almost float
They gather to bowl to each other in the nets
Where courtesies of good evening still prevail
Like "some old print",
A bitterness of engravings . . .
I'll pick my way through it

But could not imitate
The accent if I tried.

The Tower
Some years before we had rented part of a large house near the village of C. in the same county. The house had been built around a mediaeval tower fortified against raiders from across the border. The house was still lived in by the family who had been there for some hundreds of years. Their name was the same as the name of the village. In the village there was a small harbour, with a commemorative plaque saying it had been constructed by this family, in memory of one of its members who had been killed in the Tibetan Wars. The family had long-standing army connections and the part of the house we occupied was destined to become the home of one of them, currently serving in the army in Germany.

Just before the end of our stay we discovered we could get into the bottom part of the tower from our part of the house. You went through an outer and then an inner door. Over this inner door was a sign which read 'Attention! Passage of Members of Foreign Military Missions Prohibited.' This was repeated in French, German and Russian. It had been framed and a small brass plate on the frame read 'Major C. In Memory for Officially Sanctioning the Breaking of All These Signs.'

This door led into the tower itself, a high room with an arched ceiling. The floor was of enormous stones and very uneven. It was covered with a large area of spectral green mould, of a vivid emerald colour. In one corner stood a wooden chest. When opened it disclosed another chest of identical design. The label read 'Wenham Lake Ice Co.' – it was an early kind of refrigerator. A huge chain hung from the ceiling. There was one window and the embrasure revealed how massively thick the walls were – a good four feet. On the wall were two trophies; at one end a skull bearing a massive pair of antlers, and at the other an equally massive pair of buffalo horns. In their hugeness both had a primeval quality. Incongruously stuck to the wall, above the antlers, was a garish plastic Union Jack.

Northumberland

That Time in France

A dream: at the cheese counter three elderly men all alarmingly vigorous, like scrawny babies. One has a knife and is threatening to stab the woman behind the counter with it – the knife, somebody says, is 'hot'. Behind the counter there's also a pallid, lifeless figure – it's a woman sculpted out of cheese. It's supposed to be my turn now but then a woman edges in front of me, taking my place in the queue, and now she has a bowl of something in front of her. I look down at it. "Enjoy your meal" I say savagely.

To the one who is hungry inside
It is all the child's fantasy
Of 'what is inside there?'
All about what is me, what is not-me

And France, it was
Nostalgia of the other life –
Parental honeymoon, Paris
In nineteen thirty nine.

'I' is what has divided me
Where flesh once tore itself open.
To bring this about
Night after night, how those two must have laboured!

Hotel
Jug, of such thick, heavy glass –
Breast? Belly? – had shattered.
In here I am floating above the carpet.
There are slivers lodged in its pile
And I'm thinking of – eating them?
                    HOTEL OLYMPIA
Signature of this dream.
The next night HOTEL BRISTOL
A name at rest on a rooftop.
It equalled sleep.
I thought of the special bodies of children

Each in its perfect envelope of skin
And finally 'I' dreamed well.

Andouillette
At the Comptoir de Paris
Where we were almost the only diners
'Tu sais, c'est les abats'
The young waitress said, and she
Rubbed her stomach.
Slicing the sausage
I watched the guts of it
Spill out, in a soft profusion.

Midday
'Closed for lunch': walk through
Impossibly faded towns,
Voices glimpsed behind shutters.

I am thinking, what is it doing,
The words trying to find it out?
Like a blind animal's claw

The reach, the sway
Into an emptiness of air,
A faint touch, the famished presence still
As if reaching out to tell.

St Aignan
Here where time erodes
Its least important angel

In the crypt, the quiet
Moulds waiting in the earth,

Is where this other angel grew
Across the ceiling's curve

And sounds outside that I imagine
Turning to substance

Remembering who it is, will
Take itself outside,

A poor am, clothed in flesh.

At Mallenches
4.30 am is
Lying in bed
Watching sky come, breathes
Carefully, beside this breathing other.
It is no longer to get children
That we're sprawled here at noon
But as if flesh opened up
With its odd, self-emptying cry.

Late afternoon in a ditch of sleep –
There are several me's
Trying to climb out of here.

Yes that was a real You happened there,
An explosion into the landscape
Where it superintends the sun's glare.
While I was asleep beside the tumulus
(Who vomited up this spiral of stones?)
She offers a breast to the silence
While a bird goes up and down
Liquidly with its small song
And over Lozere the fraying edge of a storm.

The Bathing Place
Scar on a hillside, a heap of fallen stone,
Orchard of abandoned fruit
Grown heavy towards earth
As if what 'I' became was almost forgotten.

Here a defenceless awkwardness
Bathes itself in the
Water-lights – seeing them shine
On the undersides of boulders.

What odd hairless creatures we are,
Moving among the stones.
There's a moment of completeness
On leaving the water,

The body owning itself
In a play of light and shadow,
Is where you are being everywhere
As a breeze starts up the gorge.

The child so intent waist-deep through water,
So lightly she bears the weight of the world
And we go back up to the car,
Fossil-fuel dinosaur lumbering away.

To Resume
Time will abolish the colours.
To be at peace with the sign, it
Catches the work half-made
Statue where it lifts out of the water
                                  sets it up
Toucher c'est salir   I saw
On a sculpture somewhere
                    preserving the monument,

Or like
The faint inscription inside the dreamer's skull,
Hears how these columns are reaching up into air.
I remembered this in the cathedral.

We had entered the guts of the building
At le Puy – it was two days later –
And I found it, a dolmen slice,
Blank page of darkish stone,
Pierre des apparitions dites des fievres.
There was some light that fell
Onto it through a window of plain glass
And I thought of the analysts's couch
And some god up there, an all-seeing absence.

But still the constant
Striving to be
Here if anywhere at all
                  at Chartres

In the Gallery not much –
Soutine: 'The Artist's Hat and Brush
Donated by a former Mistress'.
A painting does have the appearance
Of being so much the guardian of silence.

Esplanade Barrouze like a roomful of trees
Breeze moss   cowbells and crucifix
Solidity of a world of objects
So carefully disposed   sit down among them
Almost as if in mourning –

Behind is the hotel
So carefully prepared for our departure.

The Dough Bowl
It was bought one wet afternoon in an English seaside town. Someone must have driven round Central Europe buying these things up, the light wood – limewood? – chiselled out by hand to make a wide, shallow bowl, and the marks this left have imparted a kind of shimmer to the surface. Acquiring it, it's as if you could buy someone else's hunger. I imagine it hanging on a wall, taking its bite out of time, something to return to and surrounding them with a sense of belonging, such as being fathered might. As well as the bowl I bought this enormous wooden ladle, and sitting inside the bowl now it looks more than ever like something out of a fairy tale. This summer we will head off once again for Europe's ragged fringes, reverse traffic moving from the centre to the edge. We'll scramble over hillsides covered in ruined terraces, thinking of the immense labour that went into their building as we watch those labouring figures where they dwindle in the fields like something seen through the wrong end of a telescope, and imagine what little we can see of ourselves in their lives, mirrors all around us turning black with time.

Here

A pale, watery bloodstain on the sheet. This is something you have almost finished with – 'like the last of the sun in the sky', you said, 'before it goes'. We get up. The tide is out. I walk over tilted fields of split rock gleaming with water and pick up a stranded starfish. The suckers on one of the arms slowly extend and contract in the brightness like drops of light. Will it live? I put it back, approach the crumbling shales. Here there are fossils. I look up, hearing slight falls of rock, each like an abrupt whisper from way above me. The stone can be split, opening like the pages of a book to show the creature inside. I find ones that other collectors have discarded. A microlite passes overhead like a giant insect. It's as if what we make and do is all imitation, flapping around this composite thing called 'world' as if just arrived from somewhere else with our words or paints, cataloguing, indexing – and here come the Open University students, in yellow helmets and carrying clipboards. 'Take care where you step', the leader says and then they all look upward, being lectured to about the rock. A man walks past jubilant because of the lobster in his pail buried under a heap of seaweed. Moving on and looking back, and thinking, 'human' is so much like an epilogue, coming along afterwards – this looking, like scavenging, as we drift across the pools of light.

There cannot in the end be any explanation for happiness. Days of such strong seeing, in the abrupt end-of-summer light, irregular stain of love, and a brief smell of blood on the wind. In the church there were black boards propped against the wall covered in careful script, biblical texts copied out three hundred years before. I looked up through the window and there is the sky and down here the writing. I thought I'd go back when the tide was out and find more fossils. I smashed open a likely looking round stone I'd brought back, but there was nothing inside. I spread out what I had on the table. Ammonite glints. It's as if by choosing one of these I say, I am chosen. It is the act of choice that creates significance. And now the ones we both found, arranged with a careful inconsequence, make a stone family.

As if something happened, and you can never be quite sure what it was or when. Alone now in the midst of all this water and light-filled space, as if 'you' is simply the echo of that distant explosion. Yesterday out on the hill I thought, this 'seeing-emptiness' is what I have, as we moved on upwards, towards a brow of hill and the approaching clouds. There was something that joined the two halves, something that was neither of us. Summer coming to an end, as I walked back into the town, and where I paused on its edge I suddenly sniffed a coal fire, sensing a first gleam of cold. So much of us is an afterwards, closing around the moment: where 'there' equals you.

Staithes, North Yorkshire

Turning

A particular moment on the stairs, a
turning movement, in which I
forget myself and in that
forgetting I almost remember.
Then the water, a downward-gushing of light.
My hands are in it like pale stalks
turning foreign and cold
for a moment, the mind bereft of itself
existing as something apart.
Shrubs outside are settling into the breeze.
There's the smell of the soap,
and the wind turns the trees again, their
green unapproachable in this dull light.
My life going on is a steady pressure
through the afternoon. There is
this elsewhere that remains unspoken
when on me, like an accent, the pronoun falls.

Hunger and Thirst

Her skirts of shadow –
She was an echo folded into sky.
I had come here
With my feelings to be plenty
But, being echo-lonely,
Was hollowed out to speak, and so became
The throat in all that flesh.

Now fruit is swollen by light:
And appetite's a blind
And famished presence.
Imprisoned here
My wholeness fades.

I am trying out my death in the flesh.
Its wrinkles are pleats of light
And here comes the child,
The one who brought famine
Home in a brightening mirror.

From so far back – a distant dress,
Its simple patterned folds.
So thirst is under cloth.

In an infant's mouth it was
Beginnings of a word
But fails in air, can't tell –
We must build upwards!

Being good at thirst gets older, it can walk in the sky.
The thirst was announced in deserts
Where it sat as if inside a mouth
Or hovering there was the answer to a mirage.

There are wells if you think them
Are days in the telling.
All this it is a translation
Of thirst's slow story passing into flesh
That had the cool warmth we'd waited on.
It is what we dreamed through thin hours.

But the well was sealed with imagining.
It returned a stone breast to the sky
Inset with small panels, a
Pictured happiness.

Analysis

A mirror, it hung
In an empty house.
Being what there was
Between me and silence
Its monotonous glass
Was miles of nothing.
Approaching it
From one side, inching up carefully
Some tendrils of breath escaped me.
A tap gurgled. Sunlight paraded
Everywhere over a floor.
Statues hovered somewhere, the
Infuriating clouds
Were slowly moving off.
But what I am trying to remember is
How, swimming up towards me
Out of nowhere, once it
Borrowed my face for a moment.

Walking the endless streets since then
Where time and distance flow together
I lie in another town,
A different ceiling underneath my head.
The mirror's a plain man telling me.
He sits behind my shoulder.
His glass is harsh
                While I remember
How once I breathed, then wrote my name
On a blurred surface, solitary tracings.

Patient

Somewhere between boredom and longing
Was where he'd felt he almost always was.
There was something that felt banished,
It moved to its place of watching and waiting
And still she was there
With that smile of an all-knowing mothering sadness
As if the light were singing in its grave.

'I want to come to him' he'd said
'From the most enormous distance'
To be a visitor there,
Travelling shaft of light that
Pauses, for just a moment,
Faint twitch of a curtain, and then that slow
Gathering of sound as the
Car, parked outside, pulls away.

So who is it lives in there now
As if baffled by his own absences –
What is it lives
In the spaces between each mouthful?
Breathing it lifts
Another page
And he can see it now.
It is the writing-self,
Me-not-me, in that
Perfected circle's pool of light –

Left long enough in here, he thought
The books will all read themselves
And looking in there I saw him –
It was Tantalus feeding.

Lyric

Each one now comes
So prompt to the breath birth –
O heave me off, she'd said,
This mass of flesh
Pinioned to window glare

And all *I* would want
Is to feed here in quiet,
This part of me, it
Eats and cries
Remembering how the blood was there.

Being bitten all over with hunger
Love is in my corner
And this, my blamed body
Its otherness has brought me here.
Listen: my hunting diamond,

The wildness of the animal
Is the sharpness of its feature,
The burnt child, this cinder child,
While kestrel hung
Like an asterisk, free-floating hoverer

Above the defeated town,
Its vegetation lurching out from brickwork
And buddleia smell after rainfall –
At rest here under the eaves of light
I'll arrive here in a small voice

Here in the city that I thought was mine,
Its bombsites where a black redstart sang
Where I found a scorched photograph.
Stories are told to bind up wounds.
But my archaic ink –

With all my words, as if
I wanted to bury something
And better this bruised lyric
Lips and throat, the heart-shaped vowels
To take my voice back home.

Leaf-touch
To ground   more
Substance needed here,

In a brotherhood of the air
To watch colour settle
Down into the trees,

Bird-claw clutch and
So on out –
It is to reach
An edge of text
            to
Taste the salt,
Brushing against her skin.

Then, that being done,
Lips complete the word.

What's gone, and now at large
Where lips complete the wound:
Tongue challenge

Being flooded with
An emptiness   as if

Such looked-for absence
Might become an answer

And what you can bring back
Inside here, into the fortress,
Token of one such day –

Stone shell feather.

A body is all hollows, bow
Stretched in air, and air
An absence waiting.

It is the shape I
Hollow here in my region
Of silences, but you knowing

Me: split image healed,
A crack joined with gold like
Lightning into the porcelain,

This coldness is a limb
Afloat on something deep who are
The skin we have to endure.

Light-hang, our
Space. It is the over-
towering lily stasis

Upholds the pond –
A lover of nothing
Parades but

Lotus cock-jewel,
The garment swish of
Water parting.

Air snapped like a flag.
I was posted to nowhere.
I am written out of my depth into light

Whose threads congeal,
Being seed   made parting
So the air dries a page.

I stir, for you
And I have to trust the words
More than I trust myself.

On an evening of rainwet fractured light,
Sun-drops peopling each bush
We'll drive further into the valley

Where the quality of the late
Light is like a released ache,
Skin-near and the

Rooks lift from treetops.
The winds take their cries.
Each leaf is the sum of light

And I wonder what this to-be-
held might be, in our quiet house
Over against the fall of dark.

The Moments

Birth-moment – was it then,
The time that I finally lost
My quality of perfect stillness?

And the strangeness of it, an
'Orientation towards existence'.
Being older now

Like the afternoon sunlight trapped in cities –
Cracked window of a self
As if consciousness were a trick of the light.

'The core of emptiness
Which is our own mortality.'
Sprung fresh from the void

Tree means, as if it were
Leaning out of itself
And onto its branch of sky.

Buddleia, its blossom's
Soft fracture, breaks
Out into our air

Here. It is the quick blur
You were made in, that moment of self.
A careful arrangement of detail

Might well be enough
Where brightness disappeared into brightness,
Infant drinking to contentment.

Salvia Turkestanica –
The long bud's like a fallen tower,
It lies on the broad leaf, held in the twist of it
Till it raises itself – there's a shining
Of very pale purple that
Darkens slightly, then opens
Into its petals, a line of small hooks.
The thick stem gets dense with hairs
That carry a stickiness, smelling of sweat
But cut with a fruitiness, acrid and sweet together
When it withers and dies. I brush
Against it now in the late, dry garden.
The seed-pods raise their arms like outworn selves.
On days like this I, being
Roused to a dazzle of air
Feel an emptiness ppening up inside me,
Great shallow heart of existence.
It is being
Quietly in your life I can almost remember.

Launched

It was a narrow door
Like a coffin lid, and swung open –
Ahead were the tight stairs.

Climbing up
There and out into birdsong, it was
Suddenly cool in the upstairs air.

Yes this room, it is something out in the sky
With a window that lifts like a lid.
My head peers out of there.

I am, being
Abruptly up
Above all of that –
The cushion of garden,
Rafts of blossom

Wing-whirr and the
Throat-swelling sound of them –
Yes, these are different doves
That land one by one on the rooftop,
Loose scrabble of claws on slates.

The giant
    Couple who are
Being found each to each
On their beds of dawn.
Beyond & outside is
The work of cloud,
It is steadily building –

Imagine: being
Freed to go
Up to that bed of daybreak
And its enormous white, being
I
   is what writes on that page

At Watch

So out quite early
With bird book and binoculars

To take a walk around himself.
Is that Start Point

Where a hawk sails its shadow
Of name across the cliff-face?

He thinks, this is such a day –
What can I do with my luck?

As the mind sails out and on to
That brightening water, it curves

Inward to where the plumages merge,
And now the names divide,

Each like a razor separating
Flesh from flesh on an opened page of sky.

Tethered to the cliff-edge and
Weighted with his book

He'll rehearse it yet again, the
Being thrown forward, plunge into the air.

It's time to go back down the hill
To his well-windowed house

In hope of meeting
A winged self coming.

Rose Mirror

Mirror sniffed its rose,
The flower of absolutely nothing.
'This is my reflection.
It is rooted in emptiness'.

A roofless building. Inside
The light's like flapping pages
And I have walked here dry as air.
I'd come here once to find my voice.

My flesh, being sailed
To a place of failing powers
Was a book that closed its own pages.
'Now it gets late', she is saying

As we sing the possible burdens.
Infinity houses the hours of us
And here I am still, one roughened
Voice come late to ground,

The god I watch shrunk to its metal
While she complains
Of a certain remoteness of feeling.
'You are too far from yourself',

Because I never see myself
Except a partial gleam.
Could I eat my way to the light?
It's still a long way there,

Us in the night and
We'll take away some of the light-stuff
From the dark place together
To freshen the sill

Where it falls, on stone and tree trunk
Or paints a facade with letters.
And so it is one rain-dark summer day
As I'm watching words and how

They fade back into the screen,
A sort of reverse etching,
I imagine one final twist of the knob
That will bring us both into focus.

The Eastern Boroughs

1
Here I am, Leyton in summer
And the light has aged me. Spill
Anywhere out of this world

Or else, just here, an edge of London,
The small quiet backs of houses.
And I am so full of it

These dinner-hours of solo walking
And a Faustian bargain's made in Leyton –
Verweile dich du bist so schon.

The sun comes palely in
And faces are
An innocence of expectation.

That tree being substance of itself's
So compact in its foliage,
Its leaves the being of summer sky.

There is the work of being
And I had thought it was words
Here among the Eastern boroughs.

2
Hidden face of a lake.
I moved my name into the sun
Feeling an odd kind of happiness

As if sunlight wind and water
Had ruffled the surface of the paint
On tight-stretched canvas

I being one for whom the act
Of reading early on became
A kind of absence.

'Like this I can grow, like a
Scar over myself', I had thought – and
'Is there enough inside me yet?'

Was this why, falling quite
Silent for a time
I fed stories in last night's dream

To the pale hungry girl inside me.
'This is quite a good thing I have found'
I'd told myself, safe in my silence.

Here I'll stay with the good things inside me
Where light embraces a threshold
And find an emptiness that is myself.

3
Is it that words build a silence
Like the fruit's dense flavour built from light?
Each Autumn I was being called

To what the winter sees
After the spectacle of leaf-fall
As if one by one they had gone

Back to their names and we were walking on air,
The crisp tread, a barely yielding
Springiness of surface.

I remember now, out walking
Into my waiting silences,
How the words when I first found them

Were flocking in libraries, something
Miraculous in their way
Of resting on the curve of a page.

4
The I of it is another, is both
Epiphany and absence –
The way it looks up from feeding, wiping its mouth,

It is an afterwards,
Something that goes on clearing and claiming distance
In the picture's painted absence.

Still I *was* there
A winged self stretched like light,
Pinned across the door.

Today out walking with you
I have come into this noise
Of wind and water everywhere,

There is something caged that
Looks for itself out here,
Something quite huge and I want it to leave me.

Remains of a tree still flush with berries
Out on the empty hillside as if
It were standing a little apart from itself.

I am feeling around inside myself
For what might be the light.
Are you here enough in the dark to find me?

You, the speaking silence,
Are making the space familiar.
You'll make me in your eyes –

Flesh and blood   behind the curtain
Owns up to being real.
So I'll grow in becoming to the world.

5
When the camera looked at Eurydice
And she hid in the photograph's shade.
She was light's image burnt into silver,

Daguerrotype mirror the light went into –
I was there too, an
Image deposit, salts drying in air

Or an ash afloat
On its small lake of light.
Image on all this shininess

Is reflection seeking its answer
Where light still writes
Its letters from the dead.

But I have flown myself out of there.
Pecking at the mirror
I dreamt my arrival,

One moment, that is, of perfect being,
Hesitant fortress
I'd said – as if sky eats its messenger.

I'll climb into myself.
You might be there too, cloud mixed
With the sunshine, to make this food real.

The Faustian bargain: in Goethe's 'Faust' the bargain Faust makes with the devil is that he will be granted one perfect moment which he would wish could last for ever.

Gallery

This city – it is
The heartfelt pause of sunlight
Out there on a piece of shaped stone.
A shadow of writing
Darkens it like soot
And we are both the tenants
Of this. But I have taken
Myself away from you
This November afternoon
And now it's starting to get dark.
 'Vase of Black Wine' is a title,
The picture tilting its silence towards me
As I wait for you to arrive.
There is a kind of hopefulness waits in your arms
Like a calm end for those of us
Who, wearing our prose selves
Will one day arrive
Separate, but together
Each clothed in our final flesh.

Benign Tumour

Our first proper holiday after my operation –
'Partial debulking' is what they call it.
We were on the beach together. You needed to cross the estuary.
Watching the ferry approach I asked if you had the right change.
Then as I was saying goodbye it came,
That moment of indescribable strangeness
Called an 'aura'. It's as if a gear shifts in my brain
And I felt I was seeing you for the very first time
Where you were standing beside me on the sand.
It was the thing still lodged in my head
That appeared to be telling me this
As you climbed in the little boat and sailed away.
I stood there for some time in the hot sun.
I watched the glittering water
Not feeling altogether well
As if 'consciousness of self' were a sort of illness
And waiting there at the river's edge I was trying
So hard to remember
How, taking me by the hand, it had brought me here.

Swift

Entered my room to a short-lived storm of wings.
How the swift got in there I do not know.
The window had been closed for hours.
Huddled there on the floor it looked up
Out of startled eyes, more animal than bird.
I opened the window and scooped the thing out
Like an insect. It sailed away,
Just a few ounces of flight this
Creature that's riskily other.
There's the way it consists of moments –
Wings and the benefit of air,
Being so suddenly there is one instant
In the afternoon-devouring emptiness.
What's *me* is something that's left
Hurtling around inside
As if I had swallowed self like an echo.
Now pressed against the window's ache of glass
It watches for that momentary return.

Lake

Bending, at day's beginning,
Over my scraps I am Tantalus
Half-buried in my waters.
Two days before
There was that corrie lake we'd found
Its silence so abruptly come upon,
The lisp and whisper at the black stone shore,
A sunless dazzle, something held there waiting.

I go out into September sunshine.
My face is hot one side and cold the other.
I walk to where the slabs of rock
Are tilted upward from the road.
It looks deliberately gardened
As if it has been waiting for me –
Honeysuckle, purple loosestrife
But all is on the fade as if
Seen in a mirror with a faint tarnish.
I turn, and watch
Today's inscrutable currents
And I strain to see you swimming to your island,
The one that you have chosen for today.
Your head's a mobile punctuation mark,
The trail you make a pale
Blemish in the water.
Now I have lost it, must imagine you
Pulling your body, seal-heavy, onto rock.

Returning home I'm at the window
Watching the sheet of quiet water
It's then I see you stretching upward –
You are unfolding in the distance like
A letter in a picture book.
Energetically you wave –
               And me? I've had to turn away
To put the words down on my page of silence.

Breathe, Then

There's more good news says Tuka
The mirror is empty
               Tukaram, trans Dilip Chitre

'Come, little mouth', they'd said
'It is expedient to breathe',
Unwinking the mirror's siege –
An infant's pronoun-rapture, seized with self

It grew itself a shadow full of words
And somewhere else the world
Being violently named.
But now there are these patient afternoons

As if the day were hiding from itself.
Going back to look, it is as if
I cannot quite remember
Just where it was I'd left it

That day the blow fell, dreaming myself awake
To an existence in the light.
I find it coming home to me again
And now I may have reached a place

Where something fatal reaches me.
I am the reader moving up behind me
Who hovers like an afterthought.
There is the storyteller in my head –

The one who rises with those fallen eyes,
The me-not-me that I'm being spoken by.
This may be as far as I
Can take him with me now.

Creeping upstairs like a child perhaps I'll
Find him thinking the sky

In a room where a mirror shallow with sunlight
Glosses the day. It empties. Outside

There is a single bird, its song
Intact, clouds wasting all the afternoon.
It will be almost the world
In there, as if that might be enough

To strengthen my faith in appearances.
Arriving, word-perfect now
And, hearing something breathe itself, I'll breathe
'Imagine living here.'

I Is

From 'he' to 'I' the pronoun –
It travelled the sky,
Being fathered: what I am heir to,
Tongue pressed against the moment

I is
A mind simply
At play with itself

And this was where
The breathing found him
Who will be up early – an old man
He waits for the sun to rise.
Years later, and I am passing my hand
Over the stone face, asking forgiveness.

Mirrored

Uncover this –
            being
it is a poor am.

We two, being
worded together

who are dusts on the mirror.

I thinks of you
Behind a window waiting
The sunlight winking back

Here being when
There is no more
Pronoun
        am
Being lifted up: one

Axe-bright moment

The Wind Harp

Aeolian Harp

This thing, that's half out in the air
With a door for the breeze to enter –
It is here, again
With its supper of winds

Textbridge

The text of a decent shame –
Don't look back at what's climbing
The invisible staircase dragging its broken wing.
It's inside you beginning to creak.
It bridges the sky
Needing a mirror to make its silence in.
There's a thick tongue trapped in its voice,
An impure sanity of flesh,
'This language, not my idea' – the book
Lifting a broken hand, the smell of its binding.

Coasting

Thinking perhaps that as the years wore on
I had come to resemble them more.
It was somewhere to hang these clothes as if the flesh
Were talking in a voice I'd simply found
Once, out on the enormous sand, the sun going down –
It loosened the sky supports and flights of gulls
Were rising and wheeling as if they were all of one mind,
Birds haunting the air for company.

Years later looked down from my bedroom
At a lawn where a number of
Large successful birds were parading about –
But to fly away and land like them?
The sky, it's a maze without ending.

But this time not to be hurried home
Turning inwards towards the dark line of trees.
A siren here sounds when the tide is on the turn.
So as not to be caught on my shrinking island
My prose is a balancing act. It moves on a sort of stem.

Sitting at my desk I had fallen briefly asleep
I dreamed I was trying to scoop the bird
Out of its cage. I reached my hands in
But it kept on edging away, as if
Something had died in my house? It was the morning after
Those tantalising marks they'd made
On canvas. It's like
Being lifted into the air, but caught
On the wrong side of a curtain.

Once inside the gallery I like to look out
Out at the window-silenced square
Before I return to the painting:

The bread is neighbour to the jug.
The light arrives with you at its china flank.
A cracked wall mirrors the painting's broken glaze.
Sun-fish royal on a plate of ice
So much unfolds out in the killing air
Its life drained away into colour.
He has tweaked it with pieces of shadow.
Paint's flourish of stillness, the snow-covered gatepost,
A surface ridged with detail. Birds lift
Against a grey sky over the leafless wood,
A lens opening opening
As if you've arrived just too late at a feast.

The bulk of me's out in the world
Wanting to know an answer, nothing profound
But reached into a surface more and more.
The voice is still hungry in the mouth,
Writing it in the shadow of words
Absurd as this may seem at such a late hour.
Sensed halfway to sleep's a shadowy benevolence
On the tide's wrong side where it's done, a remedy of shadows.

The painting described in the italicised section is by William Nicholson.

Collected

The *Collected* was in
His glass-fronted bookcase,
My clergyman father
Who'd once quoted Prufrock
Standing there in the Vicarage study –
'No I am not Prince Hamlet
Nor was meant to be'. He had said it
With such sudden feeling.
For me there were to be later
More of these spectral encounters,
Stetson, the Fisher King
And the 'compound ghost's' baked features.
Somewhere between
My father and me
It was still there, the poem. It shimmered
Over a burnt-out landscape.
It makes me think of those
Pre-dawn epiphanies
Walking to early communion,
Or his day-trips to the country –
'Sempiternal' he wrote, 'though
Sodden towards sundown',
And today as I am passing
One of those huge London churches,
St Pancras, which was my grandfather's
Parish, and I was baptised there,
I dart abruptly in,
Smell that cinnamon and chrysanthemum smell,
A sense of being there and not-there
Among the flower-dust
And patient embroidery.
I have the bookcase now
Whose fringed shelves exhale
A polished mustiness
And I remember that gesture –

Him taking it down and handing it to me,
Eliot's Collected. Sometimes I feel
It was almost the only
Connection there was between us.
Being sixty years old I cannot
Help but start to imagine
Somewhere I might return to.
Hearing his voice that speaks, out of
A sort of hesitant stillness
I hover here, make myself other
Where reflections, branches and leaflight,
Like broken water are caught
In the bookcase's glass and the sunlight
Pours uselessly onto the page where I write.
My waste lands waited then
For impossible fertilities
And it is as if I'm still saying
Give me this, give me this, the
Love that blinds, and satisfies.

Visiting Silence

Here the Doctor ceased to think in logical phrases, though words, those animated eidolons that resemble the astral entities hovering over graves, still played a part in what went on in his consciousness.
         John Cowper Powys, 'Weymouth Sands'

Orpheus
        a dust of blossom on the step
Where he turns back to check the lock
One final time.

Behind him's the absolute silence of a door
Each time he'd take the house without a word
Invisible staircase   its treads of air

In a city old to the touch
He's walking into now, upright
In March-bright windy sunshine.

His original language trapped in her gaze
He'll pass through soothing areas of of shade
To make them call their answer

But mostly it just fills spaces in the air

So what had she meant by 'forgetting the sky'?
'It's a kind of mad lyric makes me a woman' she'd argued.
'My small piece of puzzlement is the sky,
The way it takes me outside sometimes'

And how they were together
All at once in the same house
It was something neither could understand
In a world infected with grievance

Being housed here for now, each unsatisfactory presence –
'I can see myself in you all broken up'
Pursuing her
With all the varieties of unlived love.

Partnered with that other 'I am'
Was she being kept at bay or invited in?
There is something that has no outside or inside,
Is it a word? And this other

Perhaps it was an absence that he felt
On certain afternoons, a sort of pressure,
A weight of silence he could almost hear
And so he went away, but she kept saying

'That one, he's mine' posting him gifts.
I can see her now
As she walks to the publisher's door –
She's halted by a mess of reflections.

And so the dismissal. 'Of course she's completely mad'
The Orpheans playing a medley of old tunes
She was glimpsed, like disturbing a shadow
That went back underground.

North London suburb now, discreet Hades,
And if she had been visited?
Her pills set out on a tray
Are stepping stones to nowhere

'It's as if you are still walking
Fadedly beside me'.
Well, she had been brought back
From such a preposterous distance

And he had walked away
Moved into his inheritance,
Her remorseless flutter being silently trodden down.
His prospects are language-enhanced

As, taking his leave, he goes
Back to blue deserts of the air.

Commentary
Typed 'Orpheus' into google   a silent crash:
Poem ghosts I had thought erased
Were still there inside the computer's brain.
'You may have to do a rephrag'
But someone has handed me this silence.

Coin mould and coin are like fitting together
The two halves of a head
But now it is my skull
They have broken into, and afterwards
There are rooms I'm still trying to inhabit.

On anti-convulsants now
To succeed an anomalous flowering in my skull
I stepped out of the hospital
And into that selfsame square.
It was all quite familiar, and overwhelmingly strange.

The fragments I still hold
Are what I am, being broken into pieces –
'It's like this that we'll sing the best'
And look, that noble head, it bobs along
Beside its floating instrument.

It wants to go back underground
As if to find what might be still of use.
The blissful instruments were hanging there
Where she sat smiling as if pleased with death.
I felt as if

I'd left them in her lap, those faded flowers.
Standing in that doorway,
Its carpet of crumbled blossom
When I turned back one final fatal time
To look into the home I'd left

Desire for memory being buried there
And I set off this time to find
A burial ground ruled into squares –
And thought, by simply standing there
I'd let that final silence have its say.

At the Graveside

I go in through the cemetery gate and hesitate before approaching two men identically dressed in sober herringbone tweed as if it were a sort of uniform. I make my enquiry. "We're pall-bearers." I can see there's a funeral going on, the priest on the brow of the low hill, his surplice blossoming like the cumulus behind him. "Ask the gravediggers, they're sure to know." There are three of them and when I approach them and ask, two look baffled but the third seems delighted. 'Yes I've seen it.' He is an enthusiast, bounding among the graves. He begins to sound disappointed. "I know it's here. I've seen it." Has she given us the slip?

IN
LOVING MEMORY
OF
VIVIEN HAIGH ELIOT

DIED 29 JANUARY 1947

The date is wrong – she died on the 22nd. The less said the better? The sun is shining, the gravedigger is friendly, and we are tethered here under these almost motionless clouds. The headstone is beginning to topple back wards and the gravedigger says something should be done about it. He has only just started working here and intends to find out where all the well-known people's graves are. He'll look her up on the internet. He is puzzled as to why Eliot is not buried here with her.

Here is the grave, it helps itself to more sky.
The silence   it returns to you
As if it were a sort of promise made –
It was the way I chose to go
Turning towards a face of absence.
Now this stone has a satisfied stare.
It is as if its letters few in number
Are picking at the sky.
Chips of marble an all-too vivid green
Are a covering, I pick one out
And pocket it slyly under the clouds

Was this the thing he could not bear to see,
Her chaos – but transformed
Into a most peculiar stillness
And that's perhaps what terrifies
And this the silence that becomes you,
The landscape like a retreating smile

Now covered with fresh houses?
It's happening near to where I used to live
And parents, I imagine them
A pair of awkward statues
Still seated as if in a patient temple
And I being the child that noticed
What's buried turns into a name

Became someone who crept about.
And this silence now – I feel
It welcome me with open arms
Like someone breathing again.
 "Together you and I
We have been too long away."
Standing in front of it
Helpless with everything there is to say,
Such silence, it returns a sort of pride
As if it were something I'd lay claim to.

There's the patient grass as it goes in search of more air,
Someone who's turned away from breath
And this lurching stone, it's coming away
In its field in a prosperous suburb
Like a book that has only one page
But still trying to fill an emptying afternoon.
The burial place, it helps itself to the ground.

You turn and it's gone,
A mirror that swung round in the air
And found its way back into you –
Look round, she vanishes
Is restless breath against stone,
The breathing its masterpiece
And I imagined I had loved it back
Under an almost perfect sky.

Personal Poem

A woman held my tongue
So I'm not quite talking to myself.
The mother bond of speech
Was the half-scent of a word just now.
In a quarrel the one who keeps silent wins.

A poem felt like this:
An entirely new way to begin
Walking itself first thing in the morning
Over a floor patched with light
It takes me up to my room

As if it were something I'd drawn back from,
This enormous distance inside me
And I had made the stranger mine
Before it even had a name,
Opaque translation of a self

And I was finally dreaming myself awake.
Here was the shy photographer
Watching a man tread carefully round himself
Bringing the distance here,
The mirror

's impossible text.
It's the part of me that's still trying to tell you
Who feeds the mirror with lies
Afflictions of silence,
Consciousness   something freakish

Since I had breathed on the glass –
And now there's this other who breathes
Slowly like me who is filling the mirror
With life. A lyric other,
The thing it is that still lives on alone.

It can't quite help itself.
A stranger to being in words,
The afternoons it went out walking –
Over there are the tower blocks,
Their windows shrouded in sunlight.

Living what I am lived by
Like something worn on a sleeve it
Exists me up to the end,
So much of all, I is
The entry point, upright hyphen

Not quite a joiner, walks out
Early again and looks back up
At windows blank with sunlight,
Leans to the rose in someone's front garden,
It joins my breath, and I am

The instant of its scent.
I walk on down to the river.
Heron's wing shadows the water, comes down
To its station here at the margin
Where I'll hesitate to the words.

Portrait

In his journal Byron describes how the playwright Sheridan, dying, was asked if he 'would submit to an operation.' He said no, he had already submitted to two – having his hair cut and his portrait painted.

Was there something final about it
Being carried across, into a pictured silence?
Today it was simply my shadow I walked here
Hearing my footsteps as the only answer
And now I am seated in the barber's chair.
I wait here, on the edge of age, and wonder –
There might be a flask of something
Facing me on that shelf I could snatch at
Where it glints in the afternoon sunlight.
The place is shabby, it must be said.
These are barbers not hairdressers. No longer young
They came from Naples, which makes me think
Of snatches of music, farcical former kingdoms.

Blades flutter around my head.
It is like being crowned in reverse
And the last thing the barber did was to show me
The back of my head, reflection of a reflection
When, lifting the mirror, he held it up behind me.
Freud says it has something to do with being castrated
So when the time comes to pay
I'll propitiate him with a tip –
There's a little bit less of me now than there was.

But I'm thinking of someone who didn't once look back
And how he has left me seated here
Surrounded by this soft fall of hair.
He vanished into the mirror's abrupt silence
Breaking it briefly into its leaves of silver
That closed like water over him, and not even
A row of bubbles, signature of air,
To give him away. I take myself outside,
Feeling lighter now, stepping free into afternoon traffic.

Weymouth Sands

It's these spaces you are beginning to find
Opening up behind you, these gaps in memory,
Bits that fly out of your head like birds
And then disappear as if overwhelmed by sky.
The sensation is not altogether unpleasing.
This trying to remember, will it feel more and more
Like reconstructing an accident,
As if you had been living in its aftershock?
The thing is, as you get closer, one by one
The echoes disappear. Instead there are
These gaps in the fence that keep on opening up.
More and more clouds are racing towards you.
There is still that odd sensation though, of 'I am',
It hovers at the edge as if waiting
To greet somebody – the figure in mid-distance
Perhaps, who might yet succumb
To the fascination of so much surrounding absence,
The way when, a child being compelled to sit still,
You would watch the light spread its silence over stone
As if you were waiting to become that everywhere –
Because somewhere it's all still there, but
Enormously more sky.

Beached

This man, this other
Whom brilliance of sunlight almost drowns –
He is a dark blur
Out on the beach inspecting stones.
So does he come
Foolish like this each day to stare
Drawn to an edge where there is no more edge?
Something there is wears out
As if a single look of mine might drown
That figure draped in sunlight
Till given a slight lilt
It disappears and goes inside
And I had wanted it so much,
That journey here past light-infected brickwork
The train a prolonged dawdle
Towards an absence nursed by rails, and now
This congregation of small stones
To say that, being here, you are
Almost word-perfect now.

Star Fish

Language the contract
Between self and nothing
When bending to earth it
Exchanges the sky for words

Out walking on that
Uncertain estuary border
Where we found the beached conger –
It was starting to swell

While gull-flight lifted over
Ocean   pectoral surge –
I walked there a neighbour
To that small ancient heart

Tracing the shallow architecture
Text an invisible lintel
Being lifted into air, then how it
Breathed itself away

Reached home my mouth
Turned inside out
Radiant shadow
Fabric starfish.

As If Where

Birth is
Pure moment

Birth is
Pure moment

Where the sunlight falls on you –
Like an absence, is being where 'I am'

I have the remains of a voice
With the language to gather you in.

Drop Dead

No not that –
And it could be almost anyone
Just that it happens to be you

A first attempt
To banish someone watching,
Ink   the pens of others

Who's writing this? Not I?
But that relief being found
Each day's arrival with its slight reward

It's always there
A faintly irritating sound
Like wind-chimes from a neighbour's garden

Somebody out there
Who's in my skin   frail perch
Outside in the restless air.

Mask

This poor art wants to know, is the tightrope
You're walking on actually there?
The way it makes do with particulars
It walked a line and briefly

Failed to understand
Something his life tried to do.
It was the attempt as if he were shadowy bulk
Set against all that light.

The way a breeze introduced itself to the curtain –
Something moves out there
Like a voice playing with silence.
Mouth-heavy, she turns in her sleep

While beside her he breathes in that calm
Noticing age   Just soar
Autumn's dwindling
Arcades of sunlight

And now there is a faint
Upheaval in the air,
Bead curtain and eye-dazzle of broken lines.
Draw back the curtain and here he is, the reader.

Just a Touch

Such magnificent horizons are like an unfinished statement
Left 'hanging in the air'
And here they come with their carefully smoothed down poems
Multiple exchange of body fluids
That circulate in the economy of verse

An air full of broken branches
Was it meaning that kind of
Lingering sheen on the surface of the thing?
The game it played with itself
While we stood back and watched

The aim of course it was intercourse with shades,
Here at the edge the ex-fathers
In the shadow of words.
What the words bring is relief from absence
For a moment this sense of arrival.

The Thing About

it simply is
Where a statue is trying to remember itself
More and more is an echo perhaps
That waited around for an answer
'I didn't quite catch what you said.'
A performance of self?
It's using my words to remember the silence with
Till time walks off without me
It's something that makes a shape to remember us by
Only this time you are the event.
In front of a gold backcloth
The performers moved, slightly.
You turned to go and
Your pose was that moment
And it was the paint again
Like the sky all over your arms.